Media Man

BY KEN AULETTA

The Streets Were Paved with Gold

Hard Feelings

The Underclass

The Art of Corporate Success: The Schlumberger Story

Greed and Glory on Wall Street: The Fall of the House of Lehman

Three Blind Mice: How the TV Networks Lost Their Way

The Highwaymen: Warriors of the Information Superhighway

World War 3.0: Microsoft and Its Enemies

Backstory: Inside the Business of News

Media Man: Ted Turner's Improbable Empire

ENTERPRISE

Media Man

Ted Turner's Improbable Empire

Ken Auletta

Atlas Books

W. W. Norton & Company
New York • London

Copyright © 2004 by Rigatoni, Inc.

For information about permission to reproduce selections from this book,
write to Permissions, W. W. Norton & Company, Inc.,
500 Fifth Avenue, New York, NY 10110

Manufacturing by The Courier Companies, Inc.
Book design by Chris Welch
Production manager: Amanda Morrison

Library of Congress Cataloging-in-Publication Data

Auletta, Ken.
Media man : Ted Turner's improbable empire / Ken Auletta.—1st ed.
p. cm.—(Enterprise)
Includes bibliographical references and index.
ISBN 0-393-05168-4 (hardcover)
1. Turner, Ted. 2. Businesspeople—United States—Biography. 3. Sports team
owners—United States—Biography. 4. Telecommunication—United States—
Biography. I. Title. II. Enterprise (New York, N.Y.)
HC102.5.T86A95 2004
384.55'5'092—dc22
2004012215

ISBN 0-393-32749-3 pbk.

W. W. Norton & Company, Inc.
500 Fifth Avenue, New York, N.Y. 10110
www.wwnorton.com

W. W. Norton & Company Ltd.
Castle House, 75/76 Wells Street, London W1T 3QT

1 2 3 4 5 6 7 8 9 0

For Bonnie and James

Contents

Media Man

1

Getting Fired

Getting fired came as a shock to Ted Turner. He was the largest shareholder in the recently merged AOL Time Warner, owning around four percent of the combined company; his celebrated name was on the door of a major division, the Turner Broadcasting System, and his dimpled chin, gap-toothed smile, and pencil-thin Gable-esque mustache were recognizable everywhere. His life was documented by the framed magazine covers that crowded the walls of his Atlanta office: Turner in 1976, launching the first "Superstation" by transforming a weak local television signal into a robust cable network; Turner in 1977, skippering his boat, *Courageous*, to victory in the America's Cup; Turner pioneering the purchase of professional sports teams as cheap and reliable programming first for his stations and then for his cable network; Turner inventing the twenty-four-hour Cable News Network; Turner buying Hollywood film libraries to create new cable television networks; Turner as *Time* magazine's 1991 Man of the Year.

Captain Courageous in Newport, 1977. (© *Bettmann/Corbis*)

Ted Turner's business triumphs didn't end when, in 1996, Turner Broadcasting merged with Time Warner. His influence at the world's largest media company was pervasive; he played the role of the crazy uncle in the basement whose vast appetite for cost cutting had to be appeased, and in the process he helped revive the company's stock. But when, in January of 2000, Time

Warner and Turner agreed to join with the Internet company America Online, Turner was not invited to participate in the talks about the deal or how the merged company would function. He was satisfied to attend the press conference and beamed when he was hailed as a personal hero by the two CEOs, Gerald Levin of Time Warner and Steve Case of AOL.

Less than four months later, Ted Turner was fired. The news, Turner said, was delivered during a telephone call from Levin, who told Turner what Turner had often told others: the company was going to reorganize. Levin, with Case's concurrence, had decided to adopt a very different management structure from the decentralized one he followed at Time Warner. The merger had not yet been approved by the government agencies, as required, but Levin and Case decided the competition and the technology were changing so swiftly they could not afford to wait to impose centralized oversight. The company would be cleaved into two basic divisions, each reporting to a co-chief operating officer, Robert W. Pittman or Richard D. Parsons. To achieve the desired synergies, Levin told Turner, it made sense to place under the command of a single executive five divisions: Turner Broadcasting, the cable company, HBO, the magazine division, and AOL. The co-chief operating officer overseeing these divisions would be Pittman, formerly the chief operating officer of AOL. "You can't report to Pittman, so you have to have a more senior role," Levin remembers telling Turner. As Turner recalls, Levin went on to say, "Sorry, Ted, but you lose your vice-chairman title as well." According to Levin, however, Turner offered to give up his vice chairmanship in order to keep running the Turner Broadcasting division, which included CNN, TNT, Turner Classic Movies, the TBS Superstation, the Cartoon Network, his New Line Cinema studio, the Atlanta Braves baseball team, the Atlanta Hawks basketball team, the Atlanta Thrashers hockey team, and Time Warner's HBO. "I didn't fire Ted," Levin insisted. "I said, 'This is the way we need to run the company.'"

Turner did not go quietly. He protested, in a series of calls first to Levin, then to Steve Case of AOL, who was to be the chairman of the new company, demanding that he not be deprived of supervision of CNN and the other cable networks that he had sired. Turner thought that he would prevail, and in early May— perhaps because he, like Levin, hates confrontation, or perhaps because making speeches has become his accustomed mode of communication and he had now spoken—Turner got on his plane and headed for New Mexico, where he owned a 580,000-acre ranch, and where he had invited some friends to join him. Turner is America's largest individual landowner, with nearly two million acres or the rough equivalent of Delaware and Rhode Island combined. He owns twenty-two properties, in nine American states and Argentina, and he spends about half his time at one or another of them. By his own count, he rarely stays in one place—not at his offices in Atlanta or New York, not at any of his ranches—more than five consecutive days.

Turner didn't see that his travels often slowed decision-making at Turner Broadcasting. Although he entrusted most matters to a deputy, Terence F. McGuirk, he expected to approve major projects himself. AOL and Time Warner executives, however, were impatient with the peripatetic Turner. He was sixty-two, and even his friends wanted him to slow down.

He was ordered to slow down, as he learned from a five-page fax that he received while in New Mexico. The fax, a press release issued by AOL Time Warner, announced a new management team for the company, awarding Turner one of two vice chairmanships and "the additional title of Senior Advisor." The fax did not say that he had lost much of his authority, or that his five-year contract to manage Turner Broadcasting had been abrogated a year early. John Malone, the chairman of Liberty Media and an old friend of Turner's who was a guest at the ranch, recalled that when the fax arrived, "Ted went white. He was very upset. He thought it was extremely bad behavior for them to do it that way." Malone bluntly told Turner, "You can sue, but you won't get your job back. You'll just get money."

Turner's bosses tried to defuse Turner's rage by lacquering him with praise. At a press luncheon for CNN's twentieth anniversary, four weeks after the announcement, Case told reporters, "Ted Turner has been a hero of mine for twenty-five years, and he and I basically are going to be joined at the hip." Levin said Turner was "an inspiration for us" and that he would be "far more than just the vice chairman of this new company." Turner can be seduced with kind words, with pleas to work for the good of the team, but he wasn't this time. "Vice chairman is usually a title you give to somebody you can't figure out what else to do with," he said. He likened himself to a monarch in a republic.

The year 2000 turned out to be among the most miserable of

Ted Turner's life. His marriage to Jane Fonda had ended, after eight years, and this was announced in January. In addition, two of his grandchildren were diagnosed with a serious illness; he smashed his foot in a skiing accident; his beloved black Labrador, Chief, contracted coonhound disease and was temporarily paralyzed; his back hurt and he thought that he needed surgery. Most adults have the support of a spouse and family, friends, and a job; Turner didn't have a spouse, didn't have—with the possible exception of his close investment advisor, Taylor Glover—any intimate friends, and no longer ran his own company. "I felt like Job," said Turner, adding, not for the first time, that he felt "suicidal." In the new world of AOL Time Warner, it was not premature to write Ted Turner's business obituary.

2

Father and Son

The first word Robert Edward (Ted) Turner III uttered was not "momma" or "dada" but "pretty." It was an odd choice, since Turner also remembers that, growing up in the shadow of the Second World War, he yearned first to be a fighter pilot with the Royal Air Force, and then to conquer the world, like his first hero, Alexander the Great. Turner was born in 1938 in Cincinnati; a sister, Mary Jane, was born three years later. His father, Robert Edward (Ed) Turner Jr., ran a successful outdoor-advertising company. Ted's mother was a dutiful wife who tried to obey her husband's wishes. Ed Turner was a charming, gifted salesman who was on the road or at work far more than he was at home. He was propelled by the memory of his own father, a cotton farmer in Mississippi who lost his farm in the Depression and, refusing to declare bankruptcy, became a sharecropper instead. Often, Ed Turner would warn his son that Franklin D. Roosevelt and Harry Truman were communists and that the communists would take over America and execute anyone with more than fifty dollars in his pocket. For years, Ted never carried around more than forty-nine dollars.

Ted was obstreperous. He pulled ornaments off the Christmas tree and smeared mud on a neighbor's sheets that were hanging out to dry. His father instructed him to read two books each week and to eat every vegetable on his plate. Ed Turner was often drunk and would fly into a rage when Ted disobeyed; he frequently beat him, sometimes with a wire coat hanger. He would untwist it until it was straight, like a whip, and then hit his son, exclaiming, "This hurts me more than it does you." When this didn't seem to tame Ted, he reversed the punishment, pulling down his pants, lying down, and ordering his son to administer the lashings. With tears streaming down his cheeks, Ted obeyed. "It was the most painful thing I ever did in my entire life," he recalled, giving his father credit for understanding "that it would be a more effective punishment than him beating me."

Apparently, it was not effective enough; when Ed Turner joined the navy, during the Second World War, and was assigned to the Gulf Coast, the family joined him—except for young Ted, who stayed with his grandmother and was eventually sent to boarding school in Cincinnati. Ted was miserable; he was impossible to control and was suspended. When he was about ten, the family moved to Savannah, Georgia. Intent on teaching his son obedience, Ed Turner became more formal, no longer hugging his son, but greeting him with a handshake. He sent Ted off to the Georgia Military Academy outside Atlanta and then to the military program at the McCallie School in Chattanooga.

Ted read voraciously, committing poems and military history

to memory, but he hated boarding school. "I was hurt," he told me. "I didn't want to go off so young. It was like a prison. You couldn't leave the campus. There was a bell to get out of bed in the morning and a bell to go to meals, and a bell to go to bed at night." And, he added, "there were no parents there—no mom, no dad." He complained to his father, who made the major decisions in the home, but quoting from *The Charge of the Light Brigade*, Ed Turner replied, " 'Mine was not to question why, mine was but to do or die.' " Yet Turner defends and even romanticizes his harsh father, saying that he deliberately instilled insecurity: "He thought that people who were insecure worked harder, and I think that's probably true. I don't think I ever met a superachiever who wasn't insecure to some degree. A superachiever is somebody that's never satisfied." Ed Turner was intent on grooming his only son to run his business some day, and the "Spartan" regimen his father imposed, said Ted, "made me tough."

By the time he was a teenager, Ted knew that he didn't want to join his father's business. He was religious and decided that he was going to be a missionary. But, he added, "I lost my faith when my sister got ill." He was fifteen when Mary Jane, who was twelve, contracted systemic lupus erythematosus, a disease in which the immune system attacks the body's tissues. She was racked with pain and constantly vomiting, and her screams filled the house. Ted regularly came home and held her hand, trying to comfort her. He prayed for her recovery; she prayed to die. After years of misery, she succumbed. Ted lost his faith. "I was taught that God was love and God was powerful," he said, "and I couldn't understand why he would allow someone so innocent to be made to suffer so."

The experience transformed Turner. "I decided I wanted to be a success," he said. Though he wasn't much of an athlete, he became a good boxer; the same tenacity that enabled him to resist his father helped him in boxing, because, he recalled, "I could take punishment." To impress his father, he took debating and excelled at it; as a senior, he won the state high-school debating championship. He also became an accomplished sailor.

Ed Turner was constantly giving his son instructions: where he should work during the summers, whom he should date, how he had to save to pay his own college tuition. When Ted was at home, his father even charged him room and board. Expecting his son to attend Harvard, he was displeased when a rejection letter arrived. Ted was accepted at Brown, and that mollified his father, but not for long. Apart from a classics professor who infected Ted with an abiding interest in Roman and Greek civilization, in Aristotle and Plato, in ancient (and modern) military battles, Ted remained difficult. According to a detailed account of Ted's years at Brown in Robert and Gerald Jay Goldberg's *Citizen Turner: The Wild Rise of an American Tycoon*, he wasn't much of a student. He gambled. He got into noisy arguments, defending the South, defending war as a means of ridding the planet of the weak, defending nationalism. He delighted in irritating liberal sensibilities. He kept a rifle in his room and sometimes poked it out the dormitory window to fire off a round or two. He partied and drank too much. He talked about dates as if he were describing military conquests. He was a first-class jerk.

But Ted could be charming and funny and as is still the case, he was hard to miss. "I remember his voice. It was distinctive," recalled Robert S. Ingersoll, a classmate. "He was a very entertaining guy. He laughed a lot." He joined the Brown sailing team and was named the best freshman sailor in New England.

His father, who had divorced Ted's mother in 1957 and was now remarried, tried, in his son's word, to "micromanage" his life, to treat college as preparation for a business career. Ed Turner's favorite book was *A Message to Garcia*, which he constantly cited to remind his son of the soldier in the Spanish-American War whose task it was to deliver the message to General Garcia no matter the obstacles placed in his path. When Ted chose to major in classics, his father wrote angrily:

> I am appalled, even horrified, that you have adopted Classics as a Major. As a matter of fact, I almost puked on the way home today. . . . I am a practical man, and for the life of me I cannot possibly understand why you should wish to speak Greek. With whom will you communicate in Greek? I have read, in recent years, the deliberations of Plato and Aristotle, and was interested to learn that the old bastards had minds which worked very similarly to the way our minds work today. I was amazed that they had so much time for deliberating and thinking and was interested in the kind of civilization that would permit such useless deliberation. . . . I suppose everybody has to be a snob of some sort, and I suppose you will feel that you are distinguishing yourself from the herd by becoming a Classical snob. I can see you drifting into a bar, belting down a few, turning around to a guy on the stool next to you—

a contemporary billboard baron from Podunk, Iowa—and saying, "Well, what do you think about old Leonidas?"

. . . There is no question but this type of useless information will distinguish you, set you apart from the doers of the
world. If I leave you enough money, you can retire to an ivory
tower, and contemplate for the rest of your days the influence
that the hieroglyphics of prehistoric man had upon the writ-
ings of William Faulkner.

. . . It isn't really important what I think. It's important what
you wish to do with the rest of your life. I just wish I could feel
that the influence of those odd-ball professors and the ivory
towers were developing you into the kind of man we can both
be proud of. . . . I think you are rapidly becoming a jackass,
and the sooner you get out of that filthy atmosphere, the better it will suit me.

Agitated by the letter, Ted brought it to the Brown student
newspaper, the *Daily Herald*, and, as Porter Bibb reported in his
biography, *Ted Turner: It Ain't as Easy as It Looks*, the paper published it anonymously. Ed Turner had sent his son a message, and
Ted sent his father one right back.

In his junior year, Ted was expelled for smuggling a coed into
his room. In fact, this was just one of many grievances Brown
had against him. "Basically, my rebelling in college was really
rebelling against my father," Turner said. "It wasn't that I didn't
love him. He was just so domineering." Although Ed Turner was
displeased with his son's antics, he was not displeased to have
him come home and enter the billboard business. And Ted
Turner, for all his rebelliousness, wanted to help build a business

empire. Despite their feuds, Ted now rarely questioned that he would work for his father. "I liked the advertising business," he said. Most of all, he liked—no, needed—his father's approval. In this sense, his father "won" the tug-of-war. In another sense, they were twins. Both were persuasive and headstrong. Both viewed seduction as a game of conquest. Both were self-centered. Both were political conservatives. Both liked whiskey. Both battled against depression. And both had unsuccessful marriages.

In 1960, after a brief stint in the Coast Guard, Ted married Julia (Judy) Gale Nye, the daughter of a prominent sailor from Chicago, and they moved to Macon. A year later, when she gave birth to Laura Lee, Ted, intent on winning the America's Cup, was off sailing. Marriage did not stop him from carousing, and he often returned home late at night, as if in a *Playboy* cartoon, with lipstick on his collar and alcohol on his breath. Two years after they were married, Judy filed for divorce. Then she discovered that she was pregnant again, and the couple reconciled. In May of 1963, Robert Edward Turner IV was born. Ted soon returned to his earlier habits, and finally, after a sailing competition in which he rammed his wife's boat in order to win, Judy decided that the relationship was finished.

Turner was a fervent Barry Goldwater supporter and met his second wife, Jane Smith, a stewardess based in Atlanta, at a campaign rally. They married in June of 1964 and had three children in short order—Rhett, Beauregard, and Jennie. After Judy unhappily remarried, Ted was awarded custody of his two children from his first marriage. The Turners lived in Charleston, South Carolina, and Ted was not much better as a father than he was as a husband. He was "a dictator," recalls Laura, who is now close to her father. He was still in the billboard business, but because of the sailing season he was rarely home for Christmas and due to work the family took few vacations together. In the summer, since Turner thought air-conditioning harmful to the environment, he refused to install it, so the family baked. But, Ted said, recalling his own father, "I treated my children entirely differently than he did. I let them make a lot of their decisions for themselves." Like his father, however, he still made home boot camp. He, too, had sudden mood swings, and his temper frightened the children. They were expected to be in bed by eight and at breakfast before eight. Good manners were required at the table. Television was limited. If they wanted soda or candy on the weekend, they collected empty bottles to earn the money. "To show that hard work is good," Laura said, each Sunday the children would weed around the house. "He wasn't there very much, but he was always there," said Laura. "He was very loving and attentive." This is not how her younger brother, Ted IV, described his dad to Porter Bibb: "We just didn't know him when we were growing-up."

While Ted Turner concentrated on mastering the outdoor-advertising business, his father was trying to escape depression: he drank, smoked three packs of cigarettes a day, and took a huge assortment of pills. In 1961, Ed Turner sought treatment and spent a summer at the Silver Hill psychiatric hospital in New Canaan, Connecticut. A year after he left Silver Hill, Ed Turner made the boldest business decision of his career, paying four million dollars for the Atlanta, Richmond, and Roanoke divisions of

General Outdoor Advertising. Although he was not part of the decision, Ted loved the boldness of it, for it meant instant growth and power. Overnight, Turner Outdoor Advertising turned into the foremost outdoor-advertising company in the South.

Ted was convinced that they had scored a coup. His father, though, was strangely morose, fretting that he lacked the resources to absorb such a large company. He hated debt, and he had to borrow money to close the deal. His accountant reassured him, but Ed Turner was inconsolable, convinced he was near ruin, like his own father. Ted coaxed his father not to lose his nerve, but it was as if a dark cloud chased Ed Turner. The ink was barely dry on this deal, and Ed Turner was already becoming more reliant on drink, cigarettes, and pills. He returned to Silver Hill and from there placed a panicky call to a friend in the outdoor-advertising business, pressing him to buy the new divisions for the same four million dollars it had cost him. The friend, not wanting to take advantage, threw in a fifty-thousand-dollar bonus. Even after he came home, Ed Turner could still not shake his depression. "I don't want to hurt anybody. I just feel like I've lost my guts," he wrote his wife. On March 5, 1963, Ed Turner had breakfast with his wife, went upstairs, placed a .38-calibre silver pistol in his mouth, and pulled the trigger. He was fifty-three.

Turner later told Christian Williams, who wrote an early biography (unlike the two other general biographies of Turner, it seems to have had Turner's full cooperation), that he and his father "had terrible, terrible fights. It was after one of those fights—we disagreed about how the business should be run—

that he blew his brains out." He clearly had worries about Ted's business fitness. Nardi Reeder Campion, whose late husband Tom played poker with Ed Turner in Cincinnati, placed these battles between father and son in a different light: "It might be closer to the truth to recall the psychiatrist dictum *Every suicide is really a homicide*. I heard Ed Turner say more than once, 'Someday I'm going to kill that kid.' " Either way, the message was clear: Ed Turner abandoned his dreams of business glory because he felt inadequate and because he believed his son wasn't up to the task either. The son, who was twenty-four at the time, was confronted by this message: perhaps he was responsible for his father's suicide. For all that, Ted Turner inexplicably told me, "I lost my best friend."

3

The Rabbit

In the weeks and months after his father's suicide, Turner was distraught yet surprisingly focused. He told his father's advisors and bankers that Ed Turner had not known what he was doing when he resold the company divisions he had just bought; that he, Ted, would sue if necessary to reclaim them; and that, in any case, he was prepared to run the entire enterprise. His ferocity and his mastery of the numbers were impressive. The bankers came through with the loans, and his father's friend sold back the divisions he had bought.

Soon after that, Turner began to dream of going beyond the billboard business, of building a media empire. Although he owned one of the ten largest billboard companies in America, it was not a business that excited him. His company constructed billboards, rented them on a monthly basis to advertisers, paid to maintain them, and earned a profit of about thirty-five percent on each dollar. It was a nice but boring business. Turner didn't just want to direct motorists to the next gas station. "I wanted to do more with my life than just make money," he recalls. "I thought that television would be more exciting and more interesting." He had always loved movies and cartoons and thought they could carry TV viewers to magical places. Television was still a new medium, reaching a relatively small slice of the nation. It had not yet become as ubiquitous as the telephone or the radio. And television was dominated by what Turner thought of as New York elitists. They didn't love movies and cartoons the way he did. They hadn't watched *Gone with the Wind* so many times that they could recite whole patches of dialogue from it, as Turner could. They didn't police the promiscuous sex and violence that offended the surprisingly stern Turner. Ted Turner was a showman, as he demonstrated when skippering his boat to victory in the America's Cup. Billboards were too small a stage. Television would be his métier.

Three New York–based companies—CBS, NBC, and ABC—controlled television; there were few independent local TV stations not affiliated with one of these networks. Turner was a cultural conservative who hated unwholesome network programs. Since he had always loved movies, he imagined counterprogramming old movies. He also hated the violence-drenched Saturday morning shows the networks offered children, and imagined putting on cartoons like *The Flintstones* as alternative fare. He had watched from afar as John Kluge's Metromedia gobbled up independent TV and radio stations in the late sixties, and Kluge became his inspiration. Since there were still few independent TV stations in operation, he imagined running a multimedia company. "I thought we'd be called 'Marginal Media!'" he joked.

He knew that independent stations usually operated on weaker ultra-high frequencies (UHF), which meant their signals did not travel far. But the sailor who risked a wind or a different route knew that daring produced victories. Turner was determined to make money and do good, determined to take on the big boys from New York.

His first venture came five years after his father's suicide, in 1968, when for modest dollars he bought a Chattanooga radio station, WAPO. Within a year, he had also acquired radio stations in Jacksonville and Charleston. Soon he owned five small radio stations. In 1970, he acquired his first television property, Channel 17 in Atlanta, a money-losing UHF station. He borrowed heavily to make the purchase, and the consensus was that he had been outsmarted; he changed the station's call letters from WJRJ to WTCG, but this did not change the reality that it looked as if he would lose everything. "Working in UHF television at that time was like being in the French Foreign Legion," recalled Terry McGuirk, who was hired by Turner the summer after his junior year at Middlebury College and who became Turner's protégé. The staff consisted of about thirty employees; for many, the pay was thirty dollars a week and all you could eat. The finances became even more dire when Turner acquired a second TV station, in Charlotte. McGuirk, who was dispatched to sell ads, said that the new station was costing Turner fifty thousand dollars a month. And a good deal of the time Turner was away sailing, a hobby that commanded nearly as much of his attention as business did. But he managed to motivate his tiny staff, just as he did his sailing crew.

Turner charmed and wheedled to get ads, and he introduced inexpensive programming. News was alien to the man who would become identified with CNN—*too negative*, Turner complained—and at first he aired news only in the early-morning hours. Turner programmed *The Mickey Mouse Club,* Three Stooges movies, and every sports event he could find. He used his vacant billboards to promote his station. He saw himself at war with the three networks, who he said allowed "sex, violence, antisocial behavior, and stupidity" to dominate. "The networks should put a disclaimer on their product, saying, 'Watching this is dangerous to your mental health.'" Although profits were slim, he became obsessed with broadcasting. He wanted a national network, and since he couldn't afford a broadcast network (there were none for sale, anyway), he discovered a way to get one on the cheap.

Turner's and America's eyes were opened to the power of satellite communications when the Soviet Union launched *Sputnik* in 1957. The launch captured Turner's sense of adventure. "You only have one life," he told me. "You might as well make it a great one. If I'd have lived in a different time I would have been an explorer." *Sputnik* ignited his imagination. To propel an unmanned satellite into space did not just mean that the Soviet Union could spy on the United States from the safety of space. It also meant that a satellite might send and receive communication signals from earth. This would, two decades later, hold vast implications for broadcast television.

At the time, broadcast-TV stations like Turner's Channel 17 relied on microwave signals that bounced off transmission towers. Turner, however, had a tower that was twice the height of most other such towers, and his station already reached beyond its broadcast range, of forty miles, to five states. But a network of towers was expensive, and the signals were impeded by tall buildings and deteriorated over long distances. Cable had other advantages: unlike broadcasting, which produced revenue solely from advertising, cable had two revenue sources, advertising and monthly subscription charges. But cable in those days had little programming of its own; it had started as a way to improve TV reception and to extend television to rural communities that didn't get broadcast signals.

In 1975, RCA launched its own communications satellite. Gerald Levin of Home Box Office (HBO), which was then a regional cable service owned by Time Inc. that offered movies to subscribers, decided that he could transform HBO into a national pay-TV network by distributing it via the newly launched RCA satellite. All he had to do was get cable operators to invest a hundred thousand dollars in a thirty-foot dish. Turner saw his opportunity. With satellites, as HBO had demonstrated, signals could be sent across the nation. He knew that cable systems were desperate for programming. Turner could bounce signals from his local station up to a satellite, which would then beam them back to a cable satellite dish and from there to cable wires that would crisscross America and connect to cable boxes. Thus, local Channel 17 could become a national cable network—without the huge start-up costs incurred by HBO, and with an ability to tap national advertising revenues. "Satellite. That was the big step," Turner would say. "I'm like the bear that went over the mountain to see what he could see. One thing opened up another, and I kept moving on. Remember, I went from a small sailboat to the America's Cup."

The Superstation was a revolutionary insight, a way to transform a local into a national station. He could offer the fragile cable industry what it desperately needed: programming. Long before the word *repurposing* was in vogue, Turner had figured out how to extend his local programming to another channel, reusing or running it simultaneously. He would have a cause to fuel his competitive motor, for now he had an enemy. He would be aligning with the underdog cable industry to battle the dominant broadcasting industry. And he would be at war with New York and its CBS, NBC, and ABC networks, which hogged ninety-five percent of the evening television audience. He renamed the new network TBS—Turner Broadcasting System.

Turner was taking a huge business risk. He borrowed heavily and for the first couple of years sold few ads. "I was skirting financial collapse," he recalls. He did not want to fail and prove that his father was right, and this helped fuel his drive. But that was not all that drove Turner. He had no religion, yet he had faith. He believed he was destined to succeed. He does not arrive at decisions deductively; his intelligence is intuitive. An insight seizes him and he boldly follows it over the mountain.

He also took a huge political risk, since he needed approval from the Federal Communications Commission (FCC), which licensed stations to serve localities, not the nation. The broadcast networks and the local TV stations were implacably opposed, believing that cable would subvert their business by stealing viewers or their programs. The networks were joined by the Hollywood studios, which complained that Turner would be paying a local price for their movies and exhibiting them nationally, and by professional sports teams, which said that Turner was stealing their product.

Turner and others in the cable industry saw the broadcast networks—and their station, Hollywood studio, and major league sports allies—as a cartel that had induced the government to impose regulations crippling cable's ability to compete. In cable's list of enemies, none outranked the networks. Cable conventions at that time were like revival meetings, with speaker after speaker fervently denouncing this Satan. As a master salesman, Turner knew that Congress had long been concerned about the pervasive power of Hollywood and the three big New York–based broadcast networks, and he assured congressional leaders that he, a broadcaster, was trying to help the nascent cable industry provide consumers with more choices—and better choices too, since his station would not, he vowed, program violent, sexually explicit movies like Martin Scorsese's *Taxi Driver*. Of course, viewers would not be receiving first-class alternative fare, since Turner was offering movies and sports in the evening and *Lassie*, *The Munsters*, and *The Flintstones*, among other programs, during the day. The same young, underpaid employees—the "Foreign Legion" described by Terry McGuirk—worked on the Superstation. For the first time, this raw team met with national advertisers, cable executives, and government regulators. Turner was ecstatic when the FCC allowed tiny Channel 17 to become the Superstation, an overnight rival to the networks.

To the government, Turner was a champion of the people. To the infant cable industry, Turner was a savior. Cable was starved for programming, and Turner's TBS and Time's HBO became its building blocks. "The cable guys fell in love with Ted," recalled John Malone, who at the time was building the nation's biggest cable company, Tele-Communications, Inc. (TCI). Like other cable pioneers, Malone was a cowboy. He drove a pickup truck to work, wore flannel shirts, and went home to have lunch with his wife when he wasn't on the road. From his office tower outside of Denver, his windows offered a panoramic view of the Rockies. Ralph Roberts, the founder of Comcast Communications, now the nation's largest cable system, remembers the first time Turner visited him and blurted, "Do you hate me?"

"Why?" asked Roberts.

"Because you don't have Channel 17 on your cable box," said Turner.

Roberts put it on and remembered the impact on his cable systems: "We thought it was the greatest thing in the world. We had cable systems in Mississippi and it helped us gain subscriptions. He's smart as a fox. Part of his charm is to get you to help him get what he wants."

Cable was also in need of advertising dollars, and Turner made the rounds of New York ad agencies seeking to divert money from the networks, which attracted almost one hundred percent of the national advertising dollar. Chewing a wad of tobacco, Turner would barge into the offices of Ted Bates & Co., recalls Joel M. Segal, who for many years supervised all TV network negotiations. "Do any other network presidents come to your office?"

The young, dashing Turner. (© *Bettmann/Corbis*)

Turner would ask. He would ask advertising executives whether they really watched the crap on network television, vowing to offer movies they'd want to watch. Although Turner's Superstation programmed its share of junk too, he was a salesman, and he knew advertisers were eager to gain some leverage over the network monopolies. Segal had commissioned a study that found that viewers who watched HBO were best reached by a cable channel, not a broadcast network. "We advised our clients to take seven percent of each dollar they invested on the network and instead spend it on TBS." The impact, eventually, was vast. "He changed the nature of the business," said Segal. "He drew away serious money from the networks to cable. That was the beginning."

Turner began something else. To ensure continuous baseball coverage that could not be taken off his Superstation, Turner, in 1976, bought the Atlanta Braves; although he paid a bargain price of ten million dollars, he went into debt to do it. (Later, he would purchase basketball's Atlanta Hawks and hockey's Atlanta Thrashers.) Word got around that Turner was a character. He attended most of the Braves home games: he ran out onto the field to lead the fans in "Take Me out to the Ballgame"; sitting behind the Braves dugout, he'd spit Red Man tobacco juice into a cup and swill beer, in hot weather peeling off his shirt; when a Brave player slugged a home run, he'd jump over the railing and rush to home plate to greet him; he played cards with his players and insisted that they call him "Ted."

Ted Turner became Captain Outrageous. He would drop to the floor, histrionically, to beg for business; once, telling a roomful of southern ladies how to woo advertisers, he explained, "My daddy said, 'If advertisers want a blow job, you get down on your knees.'" Celebrating his victory as the captain of *Courageous* in the 1977 America's Cup, he swigged almost a whole bottle of aquavit that had been given to him by the Swedish team, and then, drinking champagne, pulled his shirt up to his neck and yelled at some nearby women, "Show me your tits!" Then he headed over to the victory press conference clutching a bottle of vodka, uttered a few incoherent thoughts, and collapsed under the table. Earlier that year, his second as a team owner, the baseball commissioner, Bowie Kuhn, suspended him for the season, accusing him of tampering when he tried to sign a player who was under contract to another team.

Turner tales became legendary. Although married, he had a roving eye. While racing in Newport, Rhode Island, in 1978, Turner coaxed a crew member, the French-born Frederique D'Arragon—then, as she was again two decades later, a girl-friend—to wait until their boat came to the reviewing stand and then jump naked into the water. Jimmy Carter remembers that when he became president, in 1977, he invited his fellow Georgian to state dinners. "He was very raucous," Carter said. "He was loud, and interrupted sedate proceedings." Carter was amused by Turner. Dick Cavett, on the other hand, was not. During a taping of his television show, Cavett pressed him, "You are a colorful, boisterous, sometimes inebriated playboy type. Maybe it's an act or it's created by the press, but that is your image. You wouldn't deny that, would you?"

"I have heard that you are a little twinkle-toed TV announcer," Turner responded. "Would you deny that?"

BY THE LATE seventies, Turner was rich, and although he still behaved in unconventional ways, he had become more serious. His travels as a sailor and his restless nature exposed him to different peoples and cultures. He had great respect for Jimmy Carter, and no doubt Carter's more liberal views impacted Turner's own politics. He began to liken himself to "an ambassador for good will." Turner realized that to continue to triumph as a competitive sailor required a nearly full-time training regimen, which neither his business nor his growing curiosity allowed, so he quit sailboat racing. He saw himself as a rabbit— "a rabbit that's small and fast. All my big competitors were like a pack of wolves, and they were all chasing me, but I was fast enough to be out in front of them." The emblem of the rabbit was stamped on Turner's brand-new Cable News Network.

For years, the networks and others had talked about but failed to act on an all-news network. It had been an idea promoted by Reese Schonfeld, a creative and prickly executive. He had visited Turner and presented the idea to him in 1978, and Turner roared his approval. He made Schonfeld CNN's first president. Turner, who was generous with his money but cheap in sharing credit with Schonfeld, told cable operators that CNN would do for the cable industry what Edward R. Murrow and Huntley-Brinkley had done for network news. CNN would make news, not over-paid anchors, the star. It would be on twenty-four hours a day, viewers would no longer have to wait until 6:30 or 7:00 P.M. to learn what occurred in the nation or world, and CNN would not be clotted with ads. Schonfeld traveled the country to sign up cable affiliates for the new network. And at most cable conven-tions there was Ted Turner, to make a speech and inspire his cable army. "He was out promoting the industry," John Malone enthused.

He was also promoting something else, a vision. "Back in the Dark Ages, only the church and politicians had knowledge, and the people were kept in the dark," Turner declared. "Information is power. I see CNN as the democratization of information."

The new cable network, based in Atlanta, made its official

debut on June 1, 1980. Ever the showman, Turner had three military bands strike up the music and had flags of the United States and the United Nations positioned behind the platform. A very nervous Turner stood erect at a lectern in a blue blazer. He was sporting a thicker mustache and Elvis sideburns and began by reciting a poem by a minor poet, Ed Kessler, that reflected CNN's mission: "To act upon one's convictions while others wait, to create a positive force in a world where cynics abound, to provide information to people when it wasn't available before." A band played "The Star-Spangled Banner," and when it ended Turner whooped, "Awww-riiight!" and CNN went live.

CNN's production values were initially amateurish—"video wallpaper," or "talking heads," network news executives sneered—and ratings were poor. Most of the work of building a staff, imposing news values, and winning clearance from local cable operators was shouldered by Schonfeld. But Turner was the galvanizer, the risk taker who dared match his money with his mouth. He practically lived in his office, hurrying through the newsroom and rarely spending more than thirty seconds with anyone. Nick Charles, a sports reporter who was one of the first people to be hired at CNN, recalled that most of the staff worked six or seven days a week and relied on portable toilets outside, and that employees would show up in the morning and see Ted, wearing a robe or wrapped in a towel, wandering out of his office, where he slept on a Murphy bed, to retrieve coffee from the newsroom. One of his executives, Steve Heyer, once walked into Turner's office and the great man was sitting at his desk stark naked. "Don't get up!" Heyer exclaimed. Turner, who then puffed on cigars, would tell them, Nick Charles said, " 'Don't worry about ratings. Just do it.' " Charles added, "He was much more than a cheerleader. He was a guy you wanted to run through the wall for."

At first, many CNN employees were dubious. Daniel Schorr, a former CBS correspondent and an early hire, was worried every time he heard Turner extol the importance of "good news," as if what he wanted was more happy news. Worry spread when, in 1982, Turner, frustrated by Schonfeld's close-to-the-vest management style and owner-like ego, abruptly fired him. Lou Dobbs, another CNN pioneer who was a business news anchor, remembered Turner as a drunken sailor and thought that he might not be "the right fellow to lead the effort." Dobbs was afraid that Turner was more an "eccentric" than a "visionary"— until he got to know him. "He felt the networks were treating the audience like idiots," Dobbs said of Turner. "He said what I wanted to hear." Of course, employees and others wondered how long Turner could sustain monthly losses of two million dollars. But these fears did not last long. "He is a natural-born leader," said Dobbs. "I once asked him his definition of a leader. He said, 'A leader has the ability to create infectious enthusiasm.' "

Over its first five years or so, CNN barely kept its head above water. It lost money, and Turner's pockets were not deep. CNN's audience grew, but measured in the tens of thousands, not millions, as did the three network newscasts. Although the networks should have worried more about cable stealing its audience, with over ninety percent of the audience now watching CBS, NBC, and ABC, this fear rarely penetrated their smug complacency.

Even when Turner fretted that he would run out of money and entered into separate discussions with CBS and NBC about being bailed out, the networks passed on the opportunity. Only in the second half of the eighties did CNN earn a profit.

CNN started as an all-day, mostly live, and mostly domestic news service. But it strayed to cover Cuba's 1981 May Day parade and a speech by Fidel Castro, and that led to an invitation for Turner to visit the island. Turner, who had never been to a communist country, and whose politics continued to soften, was curious about it, and the next year he accepted the invitation. For the better part of four days, the Cuban communist and the southern conservative hung out, smoking cigars, attending a baseball game, hunting ducks, visiting schools, discussing politics, and nightclubbing. "I never thought there was another side to the picture," Turner once said on an A&E television biography. To an associate, Turner said, "Fidel ain't a communist. He's a dictator, just like me." He learned that Castro watched CNN's signal from southern Florida; ever the salesman, he persuaded Castro to tape a promotional spot. Castro, in turn, urged Turner to take his news service worldwide. "Ted came back fired up," remembered Eason Jordan, who worked on what was then called the "foreign news desk." International news quickly expanded—CNN sent its first signal to Asia in late 1982 and to Europe in 1985. By the mideighties, when each of the networks was taken over by giant corporations that focused more on cost cutting and driving up the stock price, the networks began to close overseas bureaus. With the end of the cold war, interest in international news coverage waned. There was no Al Jazeera, no worldwide BBC as we know it today. Spurred by Turner's now fervent desire to spread international understanding, CNN became the only global news network.

Eason Jordan was the number two international news executive when his immediate boss was fired. He was only twenty-eight. Too young, said executives at CNN who wanted to dangle a fat salary to lure a New Yorker with more international experience. Jordan had never met Turner, but Turner was cheap and liked the idea of hiring a young, aggressive person with something to prove. Jordan got the job. Only Turner would take such a chance, thought Jordan. Three months later the two met for the first time. "Ted, I'm Eason Jordan," the young man said, extending his hand.

"Holy shit!" exclaimed Turner, clutching his heart and falling down.

"What's wrong?" exclaimed Jordan.

"God damn it," Turner said, rising slowly. "I knew you were young, but not that young!"

In the beginning, the broadcast networks refused to include CNN in their pooled coverage of White House events, claiming that CNN was nonunion, didn't share the same high-quality production values, and, with a much smaller audience, wanted to pay a slimmer share of the costs. Without pooled coverage, CNN could not play to its strength, which was live coverage. Turner filed a federal lawsuit in Atlanta against "the cartel" and the Reagan administration, claiming violations of the antitrust laws and of CNN's rights under the First Amendment. To build support for CNN in Congress, Turner spent thirteen thousand dollars to install a satellite dish for the House and installed cable in the office of each member of Congress. Because CNN had twenty-four hours of news to fill, a congressman had a much better chance of being seen there and of being allowed to finish a sentence. Ted Turner would win the battle for public support; more important, in a landmark ruling in the spring of 1982, the Atlanta court declared in CNN's favor.

Still another major challenge to CNN came with a joint announcement from Westinghouse and ABC that they would start a satellite news channel to provide a twenty-four-hour cable headline news service in April 1982. Turner countered by promising that CNN would launch its own headline news channel three months earlier. The battle lines were drawn, and once again the rabbit outraced the wolf. In the competition to sign up cable systems, Turner aroused his cable brethren by reminding them that ABC was a broadcaster and broadcasters wanted to destroy cable. To drive home his point, he noted that ABC News president Roone Arledge had announced that ABC's best material would not be shared with their cable partner, confirming that cable was, in the network's eyes, a second-class citizen. CNN's headline news channel received cable channel slots, and the ABC/Westinghouse consortium did not. By 1983, the presumed juggernaut surrendered, selling the infrastructure it had built and its smaller pool of seven million subscribers to Turner.

Throughout these battles Turner exhibited two qualities that were essential parts of his armor: a Houdini-like faith that a rabbit could escape any trap set by a wolf, and an I-will-die-first tenacity. "I've got a larger dose of motivation than most people have," Turner once said. "Some people are born fleet of foot and make great runners. When basic characteristics were doled out, I got more than my share of competitiveness. That's probably all. In fact, it may not be all that healthy." On another occasion, he said, "I'm like the grass. I get tramped down one day and spring right up the next. . . . Losing is simply learning how to win."

A reason for Turner's success—with CNN, with the Super-station, with buying sports teams to supply cable programming—is identified by Robert Wright, the president and CEO of NBC. "He sees the obvious before most people do," Wright said. "We all look at the same picture, but Ted sees what you don't see. And after he sees it, it becomes obvious to everyone." Turner saw that technology had made possible a twenty-four-hour network of live news, or could transform a local into a national superstation. And he knew that since the steepest cost for any station was pro-gramming, ownership of a sports team provided a steady stream of popular programming, as well as a bond to a community. Of course, he did more than see opportunity, he seized it. He was both dreamer and pirate.

BY THE MID-1980S, CNN's triumph was becoming obvious. President Ronald Reagan now invited CNN to join the other three networks for his annual year-end White House interview. As the networks shrank their overseas bureaus, CNN expanded. It invested in "flyaway" portable satellite dishes, costing about $250,000 each, that could be carried in a suitcase and used any-where in the world to "uplink" to a satellite. Turner wanted his enterprise to grow bigger still. He knew he could dent but not defeat the networks. Less than half of American homes were wired for cable; nearly one hundred percent of all homes received network broadcast signals. To dominate television, Turner dreamed of owning a network. Although Turner Broadcasting had a mere $282 million in revenue in 1984, and the New York banks spurned his request for credit, in 1985 Turner got junk-bond financing that enabled him to make a $5.4 billion offer for the so-called Tiffany network: CBS.

Knowing that he was an underdog, Turner sought political support from Senator Jesse Helms of North Carolina. Helms had mounted a campaign against CBS's "liberal bias," and he encouraged Turner to meet with a group called Fairness in Media, which had sent letters to a million conservatives urging them to buy CBS stock and "become Dan Rather's boss." Up North, many in the media expressed horror at the prospect of Turner, whom they regarded as an unsophisticated southerner, a redneck, owning the "Tiffany network." The team from 60 Minutes—executive producer Don Hewitt and his star correspondent, Mike Wallace—led the charge. Thomas Wyman, who was the CEO of CBS, questioned Turner's moral fitness to run a network and accused him of being in bed with ideological groups, although he didn't name any. Wyman and CBS, hoping to block Turner, welcomed the "white knight" financing of Laurence Tisch of the Loews Corporation, and Tisch stealthily gained control of CBS. Turner tried to fight back, but he was checkmated. CBS said it was not for sale; thus, there was no bidding for Turner to enter. First-tier investment banks or law firms were unwilling to represent the Mouth-from-the-South against the "Tiffany network" or the Wall Street–connected combine of William Paley and Larry Tisch. Turner was forced to retreat.

By this time, however, Turner was no longer the provincial portrayed by CBS. As he sought to build CNN overseas, he became much more of an internationalist; he was more concerned with saving the environment, eradicating poverty, and ending the cold war. He met and became friends with Jacques Cousteau, the primatologist Jane Goodall, the civil-rights leader Andrew Young, and the environmentalist Russell Peterson. "I was hanging around with people that cared about the future of the planet, both of the human race and of the environment. And they had an impact on me," he said. Although he had once been a smoker, he now refused to hire anyone who smoked. "I figured any young person who's dumb enough to smoke is too dumb to work at CNN or TBS," he said. In 1985, he established the Better World Society, whose purpose was to subsidize documentaries on the dangers of environmental pollution, nuclear weapons, and the population explosion. He also began to proselytize for an end to the cold war. After the United States boycotted the 1980 Summer Olympics, following the Soviet Union's invasion of Afghanistan, and the Soviet Union withdrew from the 1984 Los Angeles games, Turner financed and launched the Goodwill Games to foster athletic competition between the United States and the USSR. During this period, Turner even thought of running for president.

But to those who didn't know him—and even some members of his board who did—Turner was still often seen as a loose can-

non. They were tired of hearing that he was going to own a network or a Hollywood studio, that he was going to make movies
like *Gone with the Wind*. So when, in August of 1985, Turner,
without fully consulting his board, bought, for a billion and a half
dollars, the MGM film studio, its Culver City lot, and its library
of more than thirty-five hundred motion pictures, the consensus
was that he had overpaid. As Turner had done with CNN or the
Superstation, his decisions were based less on rigorous financial
analysis than on instinctive intelligence. He just believed that by
acquiring MGM he would be able to tap a rich supply of programming, one that might help him create new cable networks.
He couldn't prove it, and if he were a manager rather than an
entrepreneur, he probably would have given up. But he was a
believer.

The financing for his impulsive decision was arranged by
Drexel Burnham's junk-bond king, Michael Milken, who was
representing both Turner and the owner of MGM, Kirk Kerkorian. Milken reduced the amount of cash Turner needed by persuading Kerkorian to accept stock in Turner Broadcasting. "Ted
got the advice he wanted from Michael Milken, who was the
advisor to both the buyer and the seller," Terry McGuirk
observed. "Ted needed to do the deal because it gave him the
security of a steady supply of programming." The difficulty was
that Turner found himself drowning in two billion dollars' worth
of debt; he worried that he would be forced to sell CNN. Turner
saw Kerkorian and other wolves circling. Within three months,
he was forced to sell the studio and other parts of MGM back to
Kerkorian for three hundred million dollars. And to stave off

Kerkorian and other unwanted suitors, he would make a fateful decision to invite his cable partners to become partial owners of Turner Broadcasting.

Turner, however, kept the film library, and although he infuriated such Hollywood lions as John Huston and Jimmy Stewart by colorizing old movies, he also brilliantly exploited this asset. The movies became a source of cheap television programming, and Turner created new cable networks—such as Turner Network Television (TNT), launched in 1988, and Turner Classic Movies (TCM), in 1994—to showcase them. Throughout these battles, Turner never lost confidence. "If you bet against the field, you win all the time," he said. Looking back, he likens himself to Alexander the Great or Stonewall Jackson, who "hit 'em where they ain't," boasting about how he did it "right under the networks' noses" and how he managed to grow "from one-thousandth the size of the networks to two and a half times bigger." He said, "They laughed at me when I started with CBS. They laughed at me when I started CNN. They laughed at me when I bought the Braves. They laughed at me when I bought the Hawks. They laughed at me when I bought MGM. I spent a lot of time thinking, and I did not fear, because of my classical background. When Alexander the Great took control when his dad died, he was twenty years old. He took the Macedonian Army, which was the best army in the world at the time, and conquered Greece, got the Greeks to join with him, and then marched across the Hellespont and invaded Asia. They didn't even know where the world ended at that time. And he was dead at thirty-three, thirteen years later. He kept marching. He hardly ever stopped. And he never lost a battle."

TURNER DID LOSE battles. After the initial euphoria passed, it was revealed that Kerkorian had a stipulation, as part of the MGM buyback, that if Turner did not further reduce his debt within six months he would have to pay Kerkorian in Turner Broadcasting stock, and Turner worried that Kerkorian could soon gain control of his company. On top of this, companies like Rupert Murdoch's were turning a raptor's eye on the debt-ridden Turner empire. Turner was exactly where entrepreneurs and dreamers hate to be: trapped. If he did nothing, he risked losing his company. To avoid this fate, Turner, in 1987, looked to a consortium of thirty-one cable companies—in particular, John Malone's TCI and Time Inc.'s cable subsidiary—for a bailout. In return for more than five hundred million dollars in cash, Turner ceded more than one-third ownership to them; he also granted the cable executives seven of fifteen board seats and an effective veto over any expenditure exceeding two million dollars. "In hindsight, you could say that Ted lost his company," Terry McGuirk said. "But, at the time, it was in many ways Nirvana, because Ted partnered with his best customers." Turner, however, wanted to expand, and he soon learned that his new partners did not. They wanted to protect Turner's programming assets for the cable industry and keep them away from broadcast rivals. Or they wanted the assets for themselves. Turner had staved off one fox, only to allow others inside.

Turner had watched from the sidelines as, in 1985 and 1986, Murdoch formed the Fox network, and CBS, NBC, and ABC got new owners. Increasingly frustrated, he began to spend even more time away from Atlanta. Whenever he wanted to do something bold—buy a studio or a network, for example—he confronted a veto from his board. Decisions about acquisitions were made by committee. One of the few acquisitions that the board approved, in 1991, and only after Turner wore board members down, was of Hanna-Barbera, whose animation library included not only *The Flintstones* but more than a third of all the animated cartoons ever made in this country; with this library, Turner was able to create the now-thriving Cartoon Network.

When it came to programming decisions, Turner remained in charge. Betty Cohen, who joined TNT when it was still in the planning stages and later orchestrated the launch of the Cartoon Network and became its worldwide president, remembers her first call from Turner and how he bellowed, "When are we going to put on *The Flintstones*?" Turner, she said, always rejected the word *content*, a buzzword embraced by businessmen who like to think of themselves as creative. Ted understood, she said, "It's not *content*. It's *Gone with the Wind*." It's storytelling, characters, breaking news, the kind of stuff missing from the static billboard business, which is why he abandoned it. Brad Siegel, the president of Turner Entertainment Networks, remembers that when, in 1993, he was hired to run TNT, Turner involved himself in such questions as what programs provided the proper lead-ins for 8 P.M. adult dramas. "One of the great things about Ted is that he watches everything," Siegel said. "Everything we make on the entertainment side—the pilots, the movies, the specials—Ted watches everything on tape. You always got a call." And when the ratings were poor but the program was good (as when TNT aired a *David Copperfield* movie) Turner called and told Siegel, "That was the right thing to do." Turner could be cheap—underpaying employees, fighting off unions, rerunning the same movie end-lessly to pare costs. But in a way that set him apart from the new owners of the Big Three networks or most media titans, Turner understood the perils of the programming business: it was expensive, success was impossible to predict and immune to cost-benefit analysis, and a noble "failure" could do more to enhance the value of a company's brand than an embarrassing ratings success.

Turner's most visible success came ten years after CNN went on the air—with its coverage of the Gulf War. After Iraq's inva-sion of Kuwait in August and with America and Britain's threat-ened retaliation, war fever heated up late in 1990. Unlike the other networks, CNN made a financial commitment to cover any potential war from ground zero, Baghdad. Eason Jordan figured that the Iraqi communications system would be taken out in any allied air raid, so instead of relying on that system to uplink to a satellite, he recommended that CNN invest in a suitcase version of a satellite phone; this expenditure, of fifty-two thousand dol-lars, would be added to the extra millions that CNN was com-mitted to spend to cover what might be the first live war. Tom Johnson, a former *Los Angeles Times* publisher, had taken over as president of CNN on August 1, 1990, hired after a single fifteen-minute interview with Turner; the Iraqi invasion of Kuwait came on his second day at work. Johnson recalls going to Turner with various spending plans—ranging from five million to "a top plan of thirty-six million dollars." He asked Turner, "What am I autho-rized to spend?"

"You spend whatever you think it takes, pal," said Turner.

Johnson was amazed, especially because, he recalls, "I'm not even sure he remembered my name."

Johnson posted people around the clock in Baghdad and Amman and Saudi Arabia and Israel and the White House and the Pentagon and the State Department. CNN, he said, spent twenty-two million dollars covering the war. The other networks would not make the same commitment. Nor would they wheedle to keep their people in Baghdad, as CNN would. Nor would they get permission from the Iraqi government to circumvent the Al-Rashid Hotel switchboard and set up a four-wire telephone transmission from Baghdad to Amman, and then to Atlanta. When the United States destroyed the telephone system in Baghdad, only CNN had a telephone. When the Bush administration urged the broadcast networks to pull their crews out of Iraq, they complied. Tom Johnson told of how he received calls from President Bush and other government officials, urging him to leave Baghdad, and how vexing this was. When he met with Turner and told him about these calls, and about two bureau chiefs who had been killed when he was at the *Los Angeles Times*, Turner was unmoved. He told Johnson, "I will take on myself the responsibility for anybody who is killed. I'll take it off of you if it's on your conscience." Johnson added, "I, frankly, was about to order them back to Amman. . . . I clearly thought they'd all get killed."

No one got killed. And CNN's ratings rocketed. The other networks often depended on CNN's pictures. After rolling another reel on his evening newscast, NBC anchor Tom Brokaw looked into the camera and said, "CNN used to be called the little network that could. They are no longer little." Indeed. Ted Turner was on the cover and chosen *Time* magazine's 1991 Man of the Year.

Turner was acclaimed as a different kind of businessman, one who thought about more than profit margins and his company's stock price. In pioneering and nurturing CNN, said a former CNN president, Rick Kaplan, "he had an idea for CNN and that idea was not, 'I got a great way to make some money.' Some people would think, 'Oh, look how much money I can make from cable news.' I don't think his thought was, 'Here's a great way to make a killing.' I think his thought was, 'This is something that would be great for the world.' " When Turner commissioned a CNN documentary series, *The Cold War*, Kaplan said, "his attitude was: If we break even on *The Cold War* it would still be an enormous success." Of course, this airbrushes out the times Turner and CNN diminished their reputation by, for instance, turning CNN into the all–O. J. Simpson network. But Turner understood, in a way that many corporate leaders did not, that building a brand can be expensive. He understood, before his contemporaries did, that audiences would consume news differently, would want to watch it unfold live. And as channels proliferated, so would other successful twenty-four-hour cable news niche channels like Fox News, MSNBC, and CNBC. Ted Turner, who by his own estimate has watched *Citizen Kane* one hundred times, was a power to be reckoned with.

4

The Rabbit Mates

In the late eighties, Turner's personal life took a happy turn. Jimmy Carter remembers that he was hunting and fishing with Turner at Avalon, Turner's estate in Tallahassee, Florida, when Turner read that Jane Fonda was planning to divorce Tom Hayden, the sixties activist. Turner told Carter that he had always admired Fonda, as an actor and as an outspoken liberal. "I think I'm going to ask her for a date," he said. When he called, Fonda put him off. She was not yet ready to date, she told Turner, although she was soon photographed on St. Bart's cavorting with an Italian soccer player.

Turner's second marriage had ended in 1988, after twenty-four years, three children, and many dalliances. His dating patterns conformed to his travel schedule; he took up with, among others, a Playboy bunny, the female pilot of his private plane, and a CNN anchor. Usually he addressed the women who played cameo roles in his life as "honey." Turner was persistent with Fonda, and finally in late 1989 they had their first date. It was followed by

Ted Turner and Jane Fonda in 1999. (© *Despotovic Dusko/Corbis Sygma*)

many others, including an Academy Awards ceremony, a White
House dinner, and a Kremlin dinner with Mikhail Gorbachev.
They went horseback riding at Turner's Montana ranches; later,
Turner, with Fonda by his side, would point out a cabin to visitors and announce that this was where they first made love. Both
were famous, opinionated, rich, and attractive. Both loved the
outdoors. Both had endured difficult childhoods under severe
fathers who sent them away to boarding schools. Neither finished college. And both felt profound guilt after the suicide of
a parent; Fonda's mother had slashed her own throat at the age
of forty-two. "She is fiercely focused and full of idealism and,
like all of us, full of insecurities too. And so is he," the former

Colorado senator Tim Wirth, who is a friend of both, said. "She reinforced all the best qualities in him. And she said to me the sweetest thing. She said, 'You know Ted is the only person who's apologized more than I have.' They are really good, vulnerable people."

The couple held hands on Larry King's CNN program. They kissed in public. Turner brought her to CNN executive meetings and they sent flirtatious notes to each other. She got him to drink less and diet more, to abandon linen suits and spruce up his wardrobe, and to buy art for his houses. Turner's mood swings abated; he yelled less and stopped taking lithium, which he had been on for about three years because, he said, "a quack" psychiatrist misdiagnosed him as "manic."

Turner and Fonda married in December of 1991 at his eight-thousand-acre Florida estate, where bride and groom wore white and were surrounded by their children; they dined on fresh quail that Fonda had shot herself, candied yams, collard greens, and corn bread. Turner hates being alone, so Fonda moved to Atlanta. For much of the next decade, she was at his side. On short notice, she joined him on the plane to travel, by his count, to places where they never stayed longer than five days, even if it meant moving to another of his ranches in Montana, New Mexico, or Argentina. Fonda once told *Vanity Fair* that her principal priority as a wife was "showing up, being physically present." Turner needed that kind of attention. In Montana, Turner announced that he was getting rid of his cattle and sheep and returning the land to bison, the animals that grazed there two centuries ago. Fonda became an enthusiastic hunter. Gerald

Levin, who said he is "constitutionally opposed to killing animals," remembered how, on a visit to one of Turner's properties,
he learned that Fonda had shot a deer and loaded it into a pickup
truck. "I was appalled," Levin said. "It was Bambi in the back of
the truck!"

In Atlanta, Turner did not live in a grand style. He poked a
hole in the roof of the CNN Center building and put in a spiral
staircase to connect the office to what has been called a pent-
house but is really a seven-hundred-square-foot efficiency apartment, with a cramped bedroom. One wall of the bedroom was a
two-hundred-gallon saltwater fish tank, and on the other side
was the living room with one couch and two armchairs; the living room shared space with a kitchenette that was never used.
Turner preferred his favorite food, pizza; the small refrigerator
contained wine that was open and had turned to vinegar and
sweet dessert wine that he mistakenly served for cocktails. The
most striking feature of the apartment was a terrace, largely
unused, with sweeping views of downtown (for a long while,
Turner said he "was the only downtown resident—except home-
less people!"). Another striking feature was a photograph—one of
the few on display—of Ed Turner looking up adoringly at his son.
Turner had slept in his old office for a decade; this apartment
allowed him to walk to work and to order room service from the
Omni Hotel. To accommodate Fonda, he converted the bedroom
closet into a windowless office for her—"a storage closet," Fonda
called it.

"I learned a lot from Jane," Turner said. "She was his equal,"
observed Julia Sprunt, Turner Broadcasting's vice president for

communications and human resources who had joined the company in 1981 and later became one of Fonda's many Atlanta friends. "She was different. He treated her with lots of respect." Laura Seydel, his eldest daughter, explained that her father only reluctantly celebrated Christmas, thinking that it smacked of conspicuous consumption, and, until he married Fonda, did not invest time in planning family gatherings. Soon Fonda and Turner and his five children and their families had reunions twice a year, swapped Christmas presents, and attended church christenings. Laura and her husband, Rutherford Seydel II, live in Atlanta with three young children and are active in charitable activities; Rutherford worked as a lawyer for Turner. He and Laura think of Turner as a great man, but he was not always a great family man. After he married Fonda, however, Ted Turner was around more. "He's a great father," said Laura. "He makes every effort to see my kids every couple of weeks."

In 1994 during the couple's first long CNN-related around-the-world trip, remembers a CNN executive, Turner was surprised but not displeased when Fonda attracted more attention than he did in Hong Kong. Then at a banquet in the Great Hall in Beijing hosted by the Chinese government, a thousand people approached the Turner table with cameras. Turner stood up to pose when they asked to take a picture and was stunned when he was told, "No, no. We want Jane." Then in Tokyo, one thousand guests were invited to a Turner-hosted hotel reception, and he came down alone from their hotel suite and waited for her. He noticed hundreds of guests milling behind a rope waiting to enter the ballroom and ordered that the guests be let in and he would greet them. "Not a single person would come in without Jane Fonda at the door," said the CNN executive. For twenty minutes Turner stared at the motionless crowd and stewed. He had a fever and wanted to go home. Instead, it was on to India and an emergency stop at a deserted airport in Canton at 2 A.M. to repair the jet's thrust reverser and to refuel. Fonda stayed on the plane, while Turner wandered into a darkened terminal and curled up in a fetal position. At dawn, an associate found Turner, who told him of the nightmare he had just had: the Chinese mechanics would say the plane was repaired, and then it would crash in the Himalayas.

The plane will be repaired and won't crash, the associate reassured him.

"I haven't gotten to my nightmare yet," continued Turner, who felt physically miserable but couldn't resist a good punchline. "The nightmare is that the headline will be: 'Jane Fonda and others die in plane crash!' " Turner, who claims that he had a fever of 103, arranged to abort the trip and fly home with Fonda on a commercial airliner from Hong Kong.

Fonda said that Turner was never jealous of the notice she received. "He doesn't have that kind of ego," she said when this anecdote was related to her. "He put me on a pedestal. He loved my successes. He did not love my failures." Although he is not an introspective or patient man, Turner probably opened up more to Fonda than he ever had to anyone else, male or female. By most accounts, the marriage was a good one, and Turner's friends and family came to adore Fonda. Laura said, "She's grandma to our kids. She filmed our firstborn." Embraced by senior female executives at Turner Broadcasting, she went on three-day all-"girls" trips. She and Turner began to regularly invite guests to his ranches. "He's unbelievably good to the people who work for him," observed NBC anchor Tom Brokaw, a Montana neighbor. "He knows the names of their kids." Fonda may have appeared to some to be an appendage, but she was anything but. "Her influence was profound," Jimmy Carter told me while he sat in a rocking chair at the Carter Center library in Atlanta. "Ted has always been very hyper, in that he's constantly having visions of grandiose things. He was very restless . . . always dreaming. Ted told us he was taking sedatives to calm himself. . . . When he and Jane got together, Ted became much more relaxed."

BY THE EARLY nineties, however, Turner was not relaxed about Turner Broadcasting. He worried that his company was too small. He saw how the networks had persuaded the government to relax the rules that prohibited them from owning and syndicating TV programs, which is where television fortunes are made. Turner didn't own a studio, and he feared that the studios would reserve their best programs for their networks, starving Turner Broadcasting. He saw broadcasters claim, with the help of the government, extra digital spectrum space; broadcast station owners would be awarded up to six channels for every one they now owned. Since the government had not relaxed its retransmission consent rules, this meant that the networks would have leverage over cable operators, forcing them to grant broadcasters more cable channels. "I had no similar leverage or spectrum growth," Turner explained. Nor could he match the resources of NBC, now owned by General Electric (GE), in bidding for world rights to televise the Olympics, or ABC, owned by Disney, in bidding for Monday night football. To view the Olympics on two of their cable outlets, MSNBC and CNBC, the parent company charged cable operators an additional two dollars per year, Turner said. "That's about one hundred and twenty million dollars extra for them. Just like that!" Turner Broadcasting's profits doubled in the first half of the nineties, but the company got smaller compared to its competitors. The usual edge of an entrepreneur like Turner—the rabbit's advantage—seemed less vital than size.

"You need to control everything," Turner said one day in his New York office, his foot up against an empty coffee table, a bust of Alexander the Great looming above him. "You need to be like Rockefeller was with Standard Oil. He had the oil fields, and he had the filling stations, and he had the pipelines and the trucks and everything to get the gas to the stations. And they broke him up as a monopoly. You want to control everything. You want to have a hospital and a funeral home, so when the people die in the hospital you move them right over to the funeral home next door. When they're born, you got 'em. When they're sick, you got 'em. When they die, you got 'em." He flashed his gap-toothed grin and added, "The game's over when they break you up. But in the meantime, you play to win. And you know you've won when the government stops you."

Turner was not about to be stopped by government, so he grew more frantic. He set his sights once more on buying a studio or a TV network, or arranging a business partnership with one. With his friend John Malone, he tried to buy Paramount. When Viacom won that competition in 1993, Turner and Malone explored purchasing ABC, and then entered what Turner thought were serious negotiations to acquire NBC; again, some of the cable owners on his board opposed him. He had Malone's consent, but Turner couldn't win over his other large cable stakeholder, Gerald Levin, of Time Warner (Time Inc. had merged with Warner Communications in 1990). Time Warner and Levin gained a veto after inheriting Warner Communications' nineteen percent ownership of Turner Broadcasting, which was the price Turner paid for the cable industry's bailout from the choking debt he assumed when he purchased MGM. Levin voted to veto the five-billion-dollar purchase of NBC. Turner desperately tried to change Levin's mind. He always thought of himself as a great salesman, but he failed. Levin was straightforward; he explained that his corporate interests, in this case, diverged from Turner's. If Turner was seen as doing a deal that was too expensive, it might hurt Time Warner's stock. If Turner wanted a network, well, so did Levin, who was planning to launch his own Warner Bros. network. Turner thought it was too extravagant to build a new broadcast network, and it would lack the distribution strength of the strong stations owned by or affiliated with CBS, NBC, ABC, and the Fox networks.

Frustrated, Turner went back to NBC with other ideas. He courted his old friend, NBC president Bob Wright, whom he got to know when Wright ran Cox cable. Perhaps he didn't have to put up five billion? Since he was the television seer, the visionary, perhaps GE would, in effect, pay for the privilege of renting his brain and his drive? He wanted to tap GE's money reserves to acquire other media companies and become vertically inte-grated—at least until the government stepped in to stop them.

Their meeting was held at the New York office of GE chair-man and CEO Jack Welch, and was attended by Wright, Turner, and Malone. It was a disaster. "I'm supposed to be the spokesman talking about the financial structure of a deal and how it would work for both of us," said Malone. "Before I got a word in edgewise, Ted launched a seven-minute monologue." Turner discussed how he would run the company and use GE's deep pockets to acquire other companies.

"Not with my money, Ted!" interrupted Jack Welch, effectively signaling that GE wanted to be the acquirer, not the silent minority partner. They offered to make Turner the honorary chairman.

"Everyone wanted to merge with Ted," Malone explained. "No one wanted to turn control over to Ted." This was true of Rupert Murdoch, who had once gone skiing with Turner. "He is one of the most charming people you'd ever meet," Turner said. "He told me he loved CNN the way it was and that he wouldn't change a thing." Turner, who detests Murdoch, said he didn't believe him. (Murdoch declined to comment.) There was a brief courtship by Bill Gates of Microsoft. At the time, the software giant believed it needed to own content and was nosing around Hollywood and around news organizations. Gates thought that the power of CNN's brand could be transformed into an instantly successful online news site. Turner was pleased that Microsoft did not want to run the news operation, and he thought that Microsoft's deep pockets could be used to help finance a bid for CBS. But the talks went nowhere. (Not long after, Microsoft became a partner in MSNBC.) ABC also talked to Turner about a merger or acquisition, but these talks also went nowhere. Meanwhile, Time Warner was determined that if anyone was going to take over CNN and Turner's assets, it was going to be Time Warner.

When Turner is agitated, the people close to him try to wall him off from press interviews or speeches. Around this time, however, he was scheduled to speak at a National Press Club luncheon in Washington. Jane Fonda said that she was "aware of the fragility" of the relationship between Turner and Time Warner. "One false move and it would fall apart. I didn't sleep that night. Ted slept like a baby." When Turner rose to speak, he startled the audience by mentioning a story on clitorectomies that CNN had aired. Suddenly, he started comparing the mutilation of women to what Gerald Levin was doing to him. He cried out, "You talk about barbaric mutilation. Well, I'm in an angry mood. I'm angry at that, too. I'm being clitorized by Time Warner!"

"I slid under my seat," Fonda said. Levin, more diplomatically, said, "Ted is Ted. He not only says what he thinks; he gives the most amazing speeches. While I think his analogy is a little stretched, he was peeved at the time. He actually called me up and we talked about it. It wasn't a problem."

It was a problem. Turner felt fenced in, as he does when he is handed a speech to read or is told he can't do something. "My inner dream is to go to a place," he started to explain, and then suddenly burst into the old Roy Rogers theme song, "where the West commences, gaze at the moon till I lose my senses. . . . Don't fence me in." Fences loom large in Turner's mind; he hates them, and that is one reason why his landholdings are so vast. "I'm happiest when I'm on a horse on my ranch," he said.

This much is clear: by 1995, Ted Turner felt he had to escape the fence the cable industry had built around him. After thirty-two years in business, he no longer felt like a nimble rabbit. "The veto slowed me down," he said. "I knew I would fall into the pack of wolves." In the spring and early summer of that year, Terry McGuirk, representing Turner, tried to extricate Turner Broad-casting from Time Warner. "I spent about six months negotiating an exit from Time Warner and doing a deal with John Malone," McGuirk recalls. But, as much as Turner admired Malone, he feared placing CNN in the hands of such a committed conser-vative. He was also concerned about Malone's business partner-ships with Murdoch. "Ted's greatest fear was that Rupert some-how, and maybe John Malone, would wind up owning CNN," said CNN's Tom Johnson.

For all his complaints about their political biases, Turner's own biases clearly infected CNN. It was an international network that slavishly covered the United Nations, from whose vocabu-lary, by Turner's dictate, the term *foreign news* was banished, and aired documentaries on subjects Turner cared about; when Turner commissioned a documentary, he often didn't ask Tom Johnson's permission. People at CNN undoubtedly knew what the boss wanted. But CNN was not used to punishing Turner's foes, as Murdoch's newspapers sometimes did to Murdoch's foes. Turner "never once had me pull a story," Tom Johnson said. Nor, said Gail Evans, the CNN executive vice president in charge of booking guests, did he ever order executives to help a friend. "In twenty years here, Ted has never once asked me to book a guest," she said.

Meanwhile, Gerald Levin had concluded that his company was not big enough. Apart from a pay-TV service like HBO, Time Warner owned no basic cable programming channels, and in CNN Levin saw "the jewel" he could link with Time Warner's magazines, creating news magazine shows and maybe a business and a sports cable network. Just as Turner believed a missing piece for his corporation was a broadcast network, Levin believed Time Warner needed advertising-supported cable networks. Levin already had a distribution arm with Time Warner Cable, but what he lacked was the content—cable networks—to provide programming for his cable box. If Time Warner owned TNT, the Cartoon Network, or CNN, it could generate advertising revenues from the programs as well as subscriber income from monthly cable users, and gain leverage over other cable programmers since Time Warner could threaten to favor its own cable networks with lower and more desirable cable channel slots. There was pressure on Levin to do something dramatic; his company was saddled with sixteen billion dollars of debt and its stock price kept falling. To acquire Turner Broadcasting, Levin knew, would mean more borrowing and thus more debt. But since Turner Broadcasting was growing fast, it would also mean more cash to retire debt faster. It might also provide a boost for

Time Warner's stock price, which would divert Wall Streets' attention from the debt overhang. Levin knew that he had to move fast, before Turner Broadcasting was acquired by a competitor. Levin knew that Rupert Murdoch was eager to purchase CNN and was seeking John Malone's help. He also knew that GE still had designs on Turner Broadcasting. After talking it over with none of his directors and only two members of his team— Richard Parsons, the president, and Richard Bressler, the chief financial officer—Levin phoned Ted Turner in August of 1995 and asked if he could fly to Montana to discuss an "important" matter.

DESPITE HIS CORPORATE pedigree, Levin was a dreamer. He once spoke at Carlton College, and instead of giving a my-greatest-hits speech—how I rose to become CEO and a master of the universe—he talked instead of the impact Albert Camus had had on his life. Asked to describe that impact, Levin discussed the contradictory pull of Camus' work. He quoted from Camus' novel, *The Stranger*, in which the protagonist witnesses his own murder trial as if from outside his own body. "Fortunately, or unfortunately, that's what I've always felt. That I'm here but I'm actually on the outside looking at it, analyzing it, thinking about it, and when I look for deeper meaning I can't find meaning attached to the connection of events."

As a high-school student he was popular enough to win public speaking contests, to star in school plays, and to dazzle friends with his prodigious memory. He entered Haverford College as a major in biblical literature studies with a minor in philosophy, but soon gravitated toward English. We all live with our own self-images, whether accurate or not, and this is how Levin described himself to me one morning over a breakfast at which he ignored the company-supplied trays of coffee, juice, fruit, and pastries and folded one green khaki leg over the other and sipped his water: "I would get bored if we didn't have constant change. It's built into my psyche. If you lack confidence in yourself, you're going to have a tough time with change. I'm not saying that I don't have an ego, but I'm a pretty strange person. I really don't care that much about what people think of me. That's why I always thought I'd be a professor. I'm much more interested in analyzing things. As a kid, I always challenged questions. . . . The definition of change is that you don't accept anything as a given. You kind of challenge everything. The personality types that can handle that have to be very comfortable in their skin. I'm quite a risk taker. I'm willing to put everything at risk." He ticked off the criticisms he and the company had weathered during his career, and thought it illustrated this: "A willingness to put everything on the line. If you are ego-driven, you are less likely to change abruptly."

After graduation, Levin abruptly chose to attend law school at the University of Pennsylvania, where he was note editor of the law review, and after he graduated in 1963, he practiced antitrust law in New York with Simpson Thatcher & Bartlett. From the practice of law he moved in 1967 to the Development and Resources Corporation, an international investment and management company established by the legendary David Lilienthal, former chairman of the Atomic Energy Commission and Tennessee Valley Authority. Together they worked on creating entrepreneurial businesses in the Third World. The experience was so gratifying that Levin came to believe business was the proper calling for his creative impulses. He joined Time Inc. in 1972 to help develop the embryonic Home Box Office pay-cable service. As CEO, Levin made a bold decision in 1975 to jump on the back of a recently launched satellite and thus distribute HBO's programs nationally. Levin—like Turner—was present at the birth of the modern cable industry.

He became intrigued by the availability of real-time news on the teletype machine in his office. "This is incredible," remembered Levin. "I'm sitting here and I know everything that is happening every minute." Brimming with ideas and eager to move ahead, in 1977 he tried to persuade his superiors to start a cable news service. But with HBO still losing money, his elders had no appetite for this costly venture. He watched, enviously, as Ted Turner's CNN beat them to the punch in 1980. Turner made decisions; Levin made recommendations. "I was an outsider at Time Inc.," said Levin. "I was looking for acceptance." He received acceptance in 1983 when he was invited to join Time Inc.'s board of directors. He then held a succession of jobs and was being groomed to possibly lead the company, but by late 1986 the elders decided he was not CEO timber; early the next year he was removed from the board. Despite this setback, Levin did not quit. As the company's principal strategic planner, he pushed staid Time Inc. to be bolder, to seek out various merger partners. Communications companies at this time were becoming behemoths: in 1985 alone, Capital Cities Communications, with its potent television station group and newspapers, acquired ABC; Rupert Murdoch's News Corp used its Twentieth Century Fox Studios and TV station group to start the Fox television network; and GE announced the acquisition of NBC. Time Inc. was feeling vulnerable in the midst of the industry consolidation, and re-embraced Levin. Named a vice chairman and chief strategist, Levin was welcomed back as a director in July 1988. Once again he became a contender for CEO, along with Time Inc. president Nicholas Nicholas.

As chief strategist, Levin pushed for a transforming merger. He targeted Warner Communications, with its rich mix of cable systems, movie and television studios, and a music company. Overnight, Time Inc. could compete with the giants, becoming a diversified, vertically integrated communications powerhouse. In 1989, Time CEO Dick Munro and his Warner counterpart, Steve Ross, announced that the companies would merge into Time Warner. Although the flamboyant Ross shared the co-chairman title with Dick Munro and the co-CEO title with Time's Nick Nicholas, he would rule the new entity. But Ross was in his midsixties and Nicholas was anointed heir apparent. Levin was given a consolation prize: chief operating officer and vice chairman. "I said he should leave," recalled his friend, Fay Vincent, then the commissioner of baseball.

"My wife and you agree, but I think I should stay," Levin responded.

Why did Levin choose, again, to stay? Vincent, who met Levin when he was chairman of Columbia Pictures and served with him on the TriStar board, had a ready answer: "There were things he was doing he cared a lot about. And Gerry really believes, in almost a religious way, in the Time culture. He thinks it's a unique journalistic calling."

Within two years, the ailing Ross conspired with Levin to oust Nicholas and make Levin co-CEO, and then when Ross died in December 1992, Levin became the sole CEO. Still, his board was composed of Ross holdovers and many Time Inc. directors whom he secretly disdained. He added some board members and elevated his friend Fay Vincent to chairman of the nominating and governance committee, but he kept his own counsel, thinking long and intently before he made a move. "Gerry saw the board as a necessary evil," said Vincent. "I may be as close as there is to Gerry, but there are layers behind his eyes that no one gets to."

Over the next decade, Levin insisted on broadening his cable investments, and thus his huge corporate debt, at a time when the market and members of his board were opposed; he dared bet, and lost, an estimated five hundred million dollars on an early interactive television experiment in Orlando, Florida. He also bet and lost another bundle on Pathfinder, an early interactive service not unlike America Online; he watched the company's stock price plunge as he fired a succession of able executives; he watched the stock rise on reports that the Bronfman family would soon oust him.

But Levin remained a loner. When he asked Dick Parsons, a member of his board, to become president in 1995, he at first granted him little executive power. There was audible grumbling that the company was too decentralized and that Levin was too weak to confront the princes who ruled the movie, music, cable, and television divisions like separate fiefdoms. Levin lacked the charisma and the loyalty that Steve Ross—or Ted Turner, for that matter—inspired. His talents were underestimated. He was seen as too much of a nerd by the entertainment world, too much of dreamy visionary by Wall Street, and too much of a schemer inside the company. Few saw him as he saw himself: as an outsider devoid of vanity who dared to be bold.

Gerald Levin's corporate survival skills could be likened to Andrei Gromyko's, the long-serving Soviet foreign minister who joined the diplomatic corps in 1939 and over the next four decades survived many coups and government changes, eventually rising to become foreign minister. With a mustache abruptly chopped before it reached the corners of his mouth—like that of Charlie Chaplin—and with a high-pitched voice, lofty manner, slightly disheveled short sandy hair, a chin that folds into his neck, baggy dark suits, and a drab public personality, Levin did not stand out. A succession of more flamboyant executives would, it was said over the years, murder Levin—from Nick Nicholas to Steve Ross to Michael Fuchs to Bob Daley to Ted Turner. Yet he survived them all. Were cold war Kremlinologists to chart Levin's career by the position he occupied on the balcony while reviewing the annual May Day parade, said USA Network's CEO Barry Diller, they would start out wondering why Levin was in the picture, then in succeeding years they would note that Levin was in row six, then row five, then missing, then back in row four, row two, and now: "He's the only one in the picture."

ON THE EVE of his visit to Turner's ranch in August of 1995, Levin was thinking about acquiring Turner Broadcasting, and Ted Turner was thinking about selling. "I knew I was selling the company," Turner said. "And there was another reason I did it, too. I was a little bit tired." He was tired of his cable partners. He also knew that a Turner Broadcasting and Time Warner "matchup of assets made so much sense," remembers confidant Terry McGuirk. Turner Broadcasting would have the Warner Bros. studio factory to manufacture its television programs, and Time Warner's cable systems to distribute its cable networks. Turner also knew that a merger would connect Turner Broadcasting to a giant music company, the top pay-TV network in the world, HBO, and the country's largest magazine-publishing enterprise. Turner would have size, which would give him leverage. And whatever differences he had with Levin, Turner knew that Levin cared deeply about journalism, for he was a staunch defender of his magazines' independence. Turner believed Levin would guard CNN's mandate to cover the world and would not do what the broadcast networks had done—shutter overseas news bureaus.

Levin approached the visit not knowing what to expect. He had two options. One was to placate Wall Street by reducing his company's huge debt, and a way to accomplish this was to sell Time Warner's nineteen percent stake in Turner Broadcasting. The other option was to gamble and buy Turner outright, betting that the potential synergies of the two companies would excite investors. Levin favored option two and planned to say to Turner, he recalls, that only one of the four possible corporate homes then available to Turner "understand journalism, and that's Time Warner." He would protect CNN's journalistic mission.

When Levin's plane landed that morning, Jane Fonda picked him up. "You better not make my husband unhappy," she told him as they drove to the ranch. Levin assured her that his intent was to make Turner happy. Although Turner had weekend house-guests—including his neighbors Meredith and Tom Brokaw, and investor Gordon Crawford and his wife Donna—he and Levin went out on the porch alone. Levin consulted the ten or so points he had jotted down on a piece of paper about why Turner and Time Warner were a perfect fit. Turner Broadcasting, he said, "would be the pivot point in the center of the company," and Ted Turner would be a partner, not an employee. After talking awhile, Turner surprised Levin by accepting the offer. But his accep-tance was not impulsive. "When Ted got the call that Gerry wanted to visit," Terry McGuirk recalled, "his total expectation, and mine, was that Gerry had only one idea: to acquire the com-pany. Ted would never respond out of hand to something like that."

It just seemed as if Turner acted impulsively, for when he and Levin walked back into the house and Turner saw Brokaw, who had just arrived, he shouted, "Hey, buddy. We just made a deal. We're going to merge." Brokaw remembers that Levin's jaw dropped when Turner revealed their secret.

When word got out, many wondered why an entrepreneur like Turner would sell. Some believed that Michael Milken, who a few years before had served a jail sentence for insider trading, played a Svengali role, convincing his friend Turner to sell so that he could earn a monster fee. While Milken did receive a reported one-hundred-million-dollar fee that was paid by both sides, Turner insisted, "I asked Mike to help me with the transaction,

but I did it on my own." John Malone doesn't believe this. He
believed Milken convinced Turner, and then "talked to Time
Warner" and provoked the Levin trip West. Malone was surprised; days earlier he had welcomed Murdoch to Denver, where
the two men conducted a four-hour summit meeting, with Murdoch suggesting he would be willing to trade assets to induce
Malone to help him gain control of CNN. Instead, Levin had
outmaneuvered his fellow wolves. Turner phoned Malone to ask
for his blessing: " 'John, your political philosophy doesn't fit
mine,' " is how Malone remembers his friend's blunt words.
Turner went on to tell him that Levin vowed to cede the management of Turner Broadcasting to Turner, and that he would
grant Turner two seats on Time Warner's board. Malone, who
owned a sizable chunk of stock in both Time Warner and Turner,
said he would not stand in the way.

Turner had traded a silent boss for a real one. But that's not
how it felt to Turner, his employees, or to many on Wall Street.
Turner owned almost eleven percent of the merged company,
and he was not timid. Speaking of Time Warner, he told the *Wall
Street Journal* in 1997, "There wasn't the teamwork that there
should have been." He pressed Levin to sell off company air-
planes and expensive American art and to curb costs at the Hollywood studio. He stepped in to stop a fifty-million-dollar sale of
Warner Bros. movies to CBS, insisting that the Warner films
should be offered first to its own cable networks. He blocked the
sale of the company's interest in Court TV because he feared GE
(and thus NBC) would be a part owner and would compete with
CNN. He forced the Warner stores to coordinate the sale of

items from his Cartoon Network. He pushed for and won control of all new international channels, preventing Warner Bros.
from spending millions to build a staff that would duplicate
Turner Broadcasting's. He pushed for across-the-board budget
reductions, and as the *Wall Street Journal* reported, he even fired
his own son, Robert E. (Teddy) Turner, bluntly warning him over
a family dinner, "You're toast."

Whether by design or by accident, Levin began to use Turner
for his own purposes. "The edict from Gerry Levin was, 'Let Ted
be Ted,'" a Levin confidant recalls. "Time Warner was buttoned
up and bureaucratic. Ted was a breath of fresh air, and Gerry
used that to the advantage of the company." When they met with
groups of employees, he said, "Ted would get up and say, 'I've got
one suit. I don't spend money on suits. I own ten percent of the
company and each dollar you waste, ten cents comes from me.'"
Levin remembers that he was "very comfortable" with Ted's saying whatever he wanted, and had no illusions it could be any
other way. "He's the most unique person in corporate America,"
Levin said. "He's an international icon. He's more well known
than most entertainers or most government people." Levin and
many Time Warner executives were pleasantly surprised that
Turner, who is notoriously self-centered, was a team player.
Within the Turner Broadcasting group, Gail Evans said, Turner
didn't change the way he operated, except to occasionally say, "I
have to check with the boss."

No matter how many times Turner checked, however, and
even though they knew each other for twenty-five years and had
been allied in many battles, Turner and Levin never grew close.

Turner makes a point at a 1996 cable convention.

(© *Kim Kulush/Corbis Saba*)

They didn't communicate regularly. Turner was hurt that Levin, who is intensely private, never invited him to his home for dinner. They had business differences: Turner, for example, wanted Levin to fold the Warner Bros. television operations into Turner Broadcasting. He wanted Levin to assert his power over the separate movie, music, cable, publishing, and television divisions of the company. He still resented Levin's veto of his potential purchase of NBC, believing that if he had succeeded he never would have sold his company and, he added, "I'd have bought Time Warner instead of going the other way." The two men were so unalike. Levin would not hunt. He would never insult members of the executive committee, as Turner did, telling them they were too fat. He would not bridle publicly when Turner received credit as the company's stock rose, as Turner bridled when Reese Schonfeld got credit for CNN. Levin was reclusive and weighed his words carefully; the six-foot-one Turner towered over him and was impulsive. Levin was a schemer; Turner could become so focused on the moment that sometimes when he got off his horse he dropped the reins and the horse galloped away, leaving him stranded. Levin hid his vanity, while Turner flaunted his. "There are probably not two more different individuals that I've ever worked with," Terry McGuirk said. "There was not much of a connection. They ran different lives."

Ted Turner had little patience for corporate intrigue, no doubt because that's not how he scaled the corporate ladder. He respected Levin's brain—and Levin's bold vision in first pushing HBO, or now in pushing interactive television experiments. But he did not think of Levin as a leader who could galvanize his troops. In Ted Turner's army, Gerald Levin would have been a staff officer.

But events drew them together. Inevitably, perhaps, after the Time Warner merger Turner and Murdoch declared war on each other. Murdoch announced that he would launch the Fox News network to compete with CNN. Turner likened himself to Churchill and Murdoch to Hitler, and said that Murdoch had to be stopped before he took over the media and used it as a weapon to advance his conservative agenda and his business interests. Turner asserts that men of goodwill can resolve differences between, say, Arabs and Israelis, yet he does not believe it is possible to play Chamberlain to Murdoch's Hitler. "How do you make peace with a mega-maniac?" Turner said to me in a November 1996 interview. "Chamberlain tried to make peace. When you've got somebody like that, I don't think there's a spark of human decency in him—except he likes his family." Turner said that Murdoch's Fox News network would do in America what Murdoch had done in China, where he removed the BBC from his satellite system in order to gain favor with the government.

Murdoch's *New York Post* taunted Turner, describing him as a doormat for foreign dictators, suggesting that he was wacky, and portraying Fonda as "Hanoi Jane." The battle became so ferocious that executives in both camps grew concerned; after all, Fox wanted television shows from Warner Bros. and Warner Bros. needed Murdoch's satellites to distribute its programs and movies on television around the globe. Fox would need Time Warner cable systems to carry its new cable news service. And neither welcomed the bad publicity. In the end, business interests outweighed principles, a truce was arranged, and though Turner has never altered his view of Murdoch, he began to focus on other things. He had long been CNN's ambassador to the world, and as such became a familiar figure to world leaders and a champion of the United Nations and a series of causes, including banning nuclear weapons, saving the environment, and family planning.

5

A Billionaire Jeremiah

With McGuirk running Turner Broadcasting day to day, Turner had more time. And, with Time Warner's stock price soaring—Turner's shares doubled in value the first year—he also had more money. Turner would forge a new identity for himself as a philanthropist. "I want to be the Jiminy Cricket for America," he said.

In September of 1997, he was to be honored by the United Nations Association-USA, and he had the idea of giving a billion dollars—then a third of his wealth—to the UN. The Turners were flying to New York on their private plane when Ted told his wife what he planned. "I was extremely moved," Jane Fonda said, adding that she told her husband, "Don't you think you should talk to your lawyers first?" He did, and learned that he could not make the gift directly to the UN.

The next day, as UN Secretary-General Kofi Annan recalled, Turner walked into Annan's office and blurted, "Hi, Kofi. I'm going to give you a billion dollars."

"I thought it was a joke," Annan said, shaking his head in wonderment.

That night, Turner announced that he would give a hundred million dollars a year for ten years to support UN programs such as those that eliminate land mines, provide medicine for children, and ease the plight of refugees. He hired former senator Tim Wirth, who eventually recruited a staff of thirty-two to oversee the effort. Turner's only condition was that his money be used only minimally for administrative overhead. Annan remembers that Turner also said, "All of you billionaires out there, watch out. I'm coming after you."

He did, trying to shame fellow billionaires to part with their wealth. The Forbes list of the four hundred wealthiest Americans, he told Maureen Dowd of the *New York Times*, was "destroying our country," because "these new super-rich won't loosen up their wads because they're afraid they'll reduce their net worth and [wind up lower] on the list. That's their Super Bowl." He did succeed in spurring others to give, including Bill Gates, who has since given away an astonishing twenty-five billion dollars, a good deal of it to improve world health and curb the population explosion. "This has had a real impact on other donors," Annan said. "He broke the mold."

Turner has written his own version of the Ten Commandments, which he keeps on typed cards in his wallet. Without prompting, he will read from a list that includes these vows: "I promise to care for planet earth and all living things thereon"; "I promise to treat all persons everywhere with dignity, respect, and friendliness"; "I promise to have no more than one or two children"; "I reject the use of force"; "I support the United Nations."

Turner is easily moved to tears. He said of a 1996 TNT documentary on Martin Luther King, *Trumpet of Conscience*, which plays "Amazing Grace" throughout and feels more like a sermon than a biography, "It changed my life by watching it so many times. It helped motivate me to turn my life to service." Turner, who calls himself a "bleeding heart," sobbed openly when Princess Diana was killed. On a trip to China in October of 1999, with Fonda reading and CNN's Eason Jordan working, Turner put on his headphones and popped in the videotape of a popular Warner Bros. cartoon movie, *The Iron Giant*, the story of a friendship between a young boy and a metallic being from outer space who, to spare people from a nuclear attack aimed at him, sacrifices himself for the sake of the planet. Jordan remembers looking over at his boss. "Tears were streaming down his face," he said. "I never saw anybody cry like that in my life." As the credits rolled, Turner called out, "That's the saddest thing I've ever seen!"

Turner's reaction to this cartoon is related to his alarm over the proliferation and inadequate control of nuclear weapons. He is aghast, he said, that over the past half-century fifty thousand American soldiers on nuclear duty have been reprimanded for drinking or drug use, increasing the danger of accidental war. The United States and Russia still had some seven thousand nuclear weapons targeted at each other, and Turner is terrified that these—along with chemical and biological weapons—could fall into the wrong hands. He dismissed the George W. Bush administration's effort to build an antimissile defense system as madness; the technology won't work, he asserted, and, in any case, it won't prevent weapons of mass destruction from being delivered by car, by ship, or in a suitcase. All of these dangers "are off the radar screen," he said in early 2001. "We have a huge job. Probably ninety-five percent of the U.S. population doesn't know about it." And only a handful of senators do. Thus, Turner's Nuclear Threat Initiative, and his $250 million, five-year funding pledge to curb the proliferation of nuclear, chemical, and biological weapons. To co-chair it, he decided that he needed someone with standing among leading Democrats and Republicans in the United States, as well as someone with broad experience. He turned to a fellow Georgian, former senator Sam Nunn, who once chaired the Senate Armed Services Committee; a moderate Democrat, he had the ear of the establishment. Although Nunn's caution gave Turner pause, he bowed to Nunn's insistence that he be granted a free hand.

This Nuclear Threat Initiative came three years later and was not linked to Turner's UN pledge. It would, Nunn said, more than double the sum spent on curbing nuclear weapons by all the world's foundations. The task is enormous. To cite one example, Nunn said there are one hundred Russian attack submarines with nuclear reactors "just sitting there" unsecured, and Russia lacks the resources to secure them. Before educating the public, Nunn had to educate Turner and slow him down. "Ted is much more an individual who believes that the goal of eliminating nuclear weapons is achievable," said Nunn, a deliberate and non-flamboyant man whose white button-down shirts and plain ties match his personality. "I see so many things that have to be done in terms of trust and verification and transparency and stability and security before you can have a national discussion about the elimination of these weapons." Nunn advised Turner to allow him to recruit military and other leaders who don't share Turner's abolitionist views. The committee held seminars and ordered a comprehensive study to explore how it can most effectively impact these issues. Nunn said he is a Turner fan: "When he gets behind something, people know it's serious, and it's going to have the energy and resources." Most days, Turner was a fan of the cautious Nunn; some days, he worried that Nunn was fencing him in.

By any measure, Turner's philanthropic activities were extraordinary. The Turner Foundation, which he controls, awarded fifty million dollars in 2000 to environmental causes. A serious environmentalist, Turner can name every species of bird and animal on his ranches, and during the oil embargo of 1973, he sold his Cadillac and switched to more fuel-efficient cars; recently, he exchanged his Ford Taurus for a hybrid electric-and-gas Toyota Prius, which averages about fifty miles a gallon. In December of 2000, to solve a long-running dispute between what the United States owed the UN and what Congress was willing to pay, Turner joined Richard C. Holbrooke, then the American ambassador to the UN, to shape an extraordinary compromise: Turner would contribute the thirty-four-million-dollar difference, and the UN would adjust its future dues formula.

Unapologetically, Turner calls himself "a do-gooder." He says so in a loud voice, and it gets louder as he gets excited. Turner is uninhibited and is usually blissfully unaware of others; and he is hard of hearing and is too vain to use a hearing aid. "Half the people alive today are already living in what we would consider intolerable conditions," he declares. "One-sixth don't have access to clean drinking water; one-fifth live on less than a dollar a day; half the women in the world don't have equal rights with men; the forests are shrinking; the temperature's rising, and the oceans are rising, because of the melting of the ice cap." He sounds like a billionaire Jeremiah. In a hundred years, he believes, New York will be under water and it will be "so hot the trees are going to die." He continues, "It will be the biggest catastrophe the world has ever seen—unless we have nuclear war." He was outraged that the United States and others don't do more to alleviate these horrors and to combat the defense and foreign policies of George W. Bush. "The new administration attempts to make enemies out of the Russians, the North Koreans, and the Chinese to justify the gigantic military buildup it wants to make in peacetime," he said. "The economy of North Korea is smaller than the economy of Detroit! What threat does North Korea pose to us?" And he is outraged by the world's exploding population; although he has five children, he once declared, "If I was doing it over again I wouldn't have had that many, but I can't shoot them now that they're here."

6

Turner Wrestles the Bear

Turner's contradictions are as clear as his views. He is a fierce advocate for preserving wildlife, yet an avid hunter. He successfully opposed unionization at his company—"our employees didn't need another element in their lives," he said—yet he rails against elites. He has called himself "a socialist at heart" and a fiscal "conservative." He is admirably generous with his money, but cheap when it comes to sharing credit with others, including Reese Schonfeld, who brought the cable news channel idea to Turner and served as CNN's first president (and who struck back in his own memoir, *Me and Ted Against the World: The Unauthorized Story of the Founding of CNN*). He champions viewer choice, yet those who stay at his Omni Hotel in CNN's Atlanta center can only get CNN—not MSNBC, CNBC, or Fox News—on the hotel TV. Turner speaks out on behalf of the rights of women, but rarely denounces Islamic states that suppress women's rights. He has compared Rupert

Murdoch, who owns the Fox network, to Hitler, yet when asked in 2000 if he thinks Saddam Hussein is evil, he said, "I'm not sure that I know enough to be able to answer that question." And though he preaches tolerance, he has uttered some intolerant words; for example, on one Ash Wednesday, seeing the black smudge on the foreheads of some CNN staffers, he asked them whether they were "Jesus freaks." As he frequently does when he says something unwise, Turner apologized, blithely assuming that the furor would pass. It did. A week later, Turner confided, "That's the downside of speaking spontaneously."

Turner had two offices, one in New York and one in Atlanta, and they capture the odd mixture of his views: in his New York office, nearly bare, a bust of Alexander the Great peered from a shelf, while the Atlanta office, vast and crammed with trophies and artifacts, featured busts of Martin Luther King Jr. and Gandhi. "I've gone from a man of war to a man of peace," Turner explained. He offered the Turner principle of world diplomacy: "Just about everybody will be friendly toward us if we are friendly with them." No issue, not even the Middle East, is intractable to Ted Turner. "They did it in South Africa," he explained when asked about Arab and Jew.

Despite Turner's success, people who meet him often think that he is peculiar. They hear his piercing laugh and the long *Ahhhhhhhhhhhh* he utters as he pauses between words or thoughts, which veer off in surprising directions, and they have no other explanation. A former director of Turner Broadcasting's board who counts himself a friend and a fan describes Turner as a fascinating amalgam of opposites: "He's a mixture of a genius and a jackass. I think Ted could have run for president of the United States—if there were not the jackass side."

The jackass side of Turner appears because, he himself says, "I don't have any idea what I'm going to say. I say what comes to my mind." Gerald Levin put it in the best light: "Ted is by far the most interesting person I've ever met—how he reacts to things. It's as if a child were speaking without any social inhibitions. . . . He'll just speak out loud what may be going through someone's mind, and he'll say it to everybody. I think that's a beautiful characteristic. He's angelic. The whole world is socially constrained. I love and respect this about Ted, but for other people it may be very difficult."

Surely how Turner reacts was more difficult for Levin than he let on, as it was more difficult for members of the Friars Club, who honored Turner in November of 1996 at a lifetime-achievement black-tie dinner. After he received his award and made a short speech, the lights dimmed, and then, as various entertainers, including the comedian Alan King, prepared to toast him, Turner, who insists on getting to bed early, grabbed Fonda's arm and departed, leaving the crowd gasping and King bellowing, "Rupert Murdoch was right—you are nuts!"

On other occasions, Turner's humor redeemed the situation. In January of 1999, he was invited to address the American Chamber of Commerce in Berlin. Eason Jordan, who oversaw international coverage for CNN, had briefed Turner on what he shouldn't say to his audience, made up largely of Germans. Nevertheless, Jordan recalled, the CNN staff was nervous because

"I lose my self-restraint and . . . just get up and dance sometimes."
Soon after he purchased the Atlanta Braves, Turner danced on the
field to celebrate the end of a 13-game losing streak. (© *Bettmann/Corbis*)

Turner decided to forgo prepared remarks and had said, "I'll wing it." And he did.

"You know, you Germans had a bad century," Turner declared. "You were on the wrong side of two wars. You were the losers."

Jordan remembers, "I went under the table." This was not an unusual reaction, for Turner likes to say he doesn't prepare: "I don't have any idea what I'm going to say. I say what comes to my mind." Above all, he said, he doesn't want to bore himself, and by not knowing what he's going to say, he ensures this. His associates worried, as they often did, whether this speech in Berlin would be still another occasion for Turner to later offer an apology for offending his audience, as he's done to American Indians, Italians, Greeks, Russians, Jews, Catholics, Poles, born-again Christians, and right-to-lifers, whom he once called "bozos."

Winging it, Turner continued: "I know what that's like. When I bought the Atlanta Braves, we couldn't win either. You guys can turn it around. You can start making the right choices. If the Atlanta Braves could do it, then Germany can do it." The audience laughed with Turner, not at him. He flashed his gap-toothed smile and left the podium to a standing ovation. He walked over to Jordan, threw an arm around him, and said, "I did exactly what you told me not to do!"

Turner likens his behavior to Zorba the Greek: "I lose my self-restraint and . . . just get up and dance sometimes."

TURNER MAY CHAMPION disarmament, but not when it comes to Rupert Murdoch. When the owners of the Los Angeles Dodgers announced their intention to sell the baseball team to Murdoch in early 1998, Turner mounted a crusade among fellow owners to try and block the sale, saying Murdoch didn't love the game and was a mercenary. Turner attracted the support of just one other owner. This did not prevent Turner from continuing to denounce Murdoch as a malignancy on journalism. Thus, Turner was especially embarrassed when CNN, in June of 1998, was accused of politicizing its news. The issue flared soon after CNN and three Time Inc. publications—*Time*, *Fortune*, and *Enter-*

tainment Weekly—started joint weekly magazine shows. The joint effort, they believed, would boost ratings while breaking news in two mediums, television and the magazines. The inaugural magazine show with *Time* asserted that American forces secretly employed sarin or poison gas in Laos during the Vietnam War, hoping to harm American or other defectors, in what was called "Operation Tailwind." The U.S. military, they reported, covered up this operation. It made for a sensational debut— except CNN and *Time* later decided it wasn't true and issued a retraction. It led to terminations and reprimands and to Turner histrionically telling reporters, "It's been the most horrible nightmare I've ever lived through. . . . If committing suicide would help, I've even given that some consideration."

Turner had more reason to feel suicidal at the start of 2000. Tension had been building in his marriage. Fonda began spending more time in Atlanta and less time with him. She wanted to be with her daughter, Vanessa Vadim, who had moved to Atlanta and was raising a child on her own. Fonda's daughter Lulu, whose father was a Black Panther, and whom Jane took in when she and Tom Hayden ran a California children's camp for troubled kids, had also moved to Atlanta. In addition, Fonda had started the Georgia Campaign for Adolescent Pregnancy Prevention and had taken up the cause of nurturing teen mothers. During this time, according to an E! biography of Fonda that aired in October of 2000, she started attending services at the Providence Missionary Baptist Church and became a hymn-singing, praise-the-Lord evangelist. Turner, who alternately describes himself as an atheist and an agnostic, told me his reaction: "I had

absolutely no warning about it. She didn't tell me she was thinking about doing it. She just came home and said, 'I've become a
born-again Christian.' Before that, she was not a religious person.
That's a pretty big change for your wife of nine years to tell you.
That's a shock. I mean, normally that's the kind of thing your wife
or husband would discuss with you before they did it or while
they were thinking about it. . . . Obviously, we weren't commu-
nicating very well at that time."

"My becoming a Christian upset him very much—for good
reason," Fonda said. "He's my husband and I chose not to discuss
it with him—because he would have talked me out of it. He's a
debating champion. He saw it as writing on the wall. And it was
about other things. He knew my daughter was having a baby and
it would take me away from him. He needs someone to be there
one hundred percent of the time. He thinks that's love. It is not
love. It's babysitting. I didn't want to tell you this. We went in
different directions. I grew up." Turner's daughter Laura doesn't
think religion per se was the nub of their disagreement. She said,
"It was another male"—Jesus. "It took time away from him."

There were other differences, friends of both say, including
Turner's libido and his insecurities. "If I got divorced," Turner
once told *Modern Maturity* magazine, "I'd probably get married
again. I'll marry the first person who comes along. My problem
is, I love every woman I meet." He and Fonda visited marriage
counselors and psychiatrists, to no avail. On January 4, 2000,
they announced an official separation. Before the separation was
announced, Frederique D'Arragon, fifty-one, who had been in
and out of Turner's life for more than thirty years, came back into

it. Petite, at five-foot-five, and shapely, she prefers jeans to designer dresses and speaks several languages. Soon after the separation, Fonda and D'Arragon lunched in Atlanta. Fonda understood that D'Arragon would be available for Turner in ways she no longer could be: "He needs to be taken care of. She has no children. And she's loved him a long time."

A close friend, who described Turner as "a great human being," said that he is burdened by three curses: an insecurity that can be traced back to his abusive father; a manic, restless nature; and lust. "Each one of these is a great huge bear," the friend said. "Turner must wrestle with three bears, and they sometimes overwhelm him." Fonda put it another way: "Why this guy didn't go under psychologically at age five, I don't know. It scarred him for life. It colors everything—his relationships, his anxieties . . ."

Fonda and Turner insisted that they still loved each other; both friends and family were distressed by their split. But Fonda, despite her own notoriety as an actor and as a political activist, had lived in the shadow of three dominant husbands. By leaving Turner, she also announced her own liberation.

7

The Merger from Hell

Turner was despondent, and his sense of abandonment was heightened by the January 10, 2000, announcement that Time Warner was merging with AOL—more accurately, AOL was acquiring Time Warner, since AOL claimed the majority of stock in the new company. The price, based on the stock values of the companies on the day of the announcement, was pegged at $165 billion, the largest corporate marriage ever. Although Turner owned about ten percent of Time Warner and as a board member had been alerted to the merger discussions, he had not been invited by Gerald Levin to participate. "Ted was not a strategic partner," a senior executive at Time Warner who is close to Turner said. "Gerry is a sole practitioner. He keeps things to himself."

Levin's decision to merge with AOL, like his decision to acquire Turner Broadcasting, was done with minimum consultation. He conferred only with Richard Parsons, then chief financial officer Richard Bressler, and a few select directors like Fay

From left to right: Michael Kelly, Bob Pittman, Steve Case, Gerald Levin, Ted Turner, and Richard Parsons at the announcement of the merger of AOL and Time Warner, January 10, 2000. (© Stone Les/Corbis Sygma)

Vincent, before agreeing to merge with AOL. He uttered not a word of the idea to Ted Turner before he told the board. In less than two months, Levin and the AOL chairman Steve Case reached agreement. To Levin, AOL was that rare company that had figured out how to make money off the Internet. It served as the gateway to the Web for half of all Americans that went online. In the new medium of the Internet, AOL could be the engine to promote and sell Time Warner's magazines, music, movies, books, and television shows. It enjoyed multiple sources of revenues—monthly subscriptions, advertising, and e-commerce. AOL, at last, solved the Internet puzzle Gerald Levin had lost millions trying to master. AOL, Levin thought, would transform Time Warner from an old to a new media company.

To Steve Case, AOL had weaknesses Time Warner might cure. AOL was in danger of becoming a classic middleman, since it owned neither the telephone or cable wires that connected its subscribers to the Internet, nor the kind of rich content that would keep them coming back. How long would subscribers pay more than twenty dollars per month to AOL for e-mail or other services they might get more cheaply? Time Warner provided AOL with distribution through its cable wires. It offered the kind of content AOL lacked, including access to abundant libraries of films, music, books, and television programs.

With AOL's stock hovering above seventy dollars per share, Steve Case wanted to exploit his inflated currency to purchase a media company with rich content. He had approached others, including Sumner Redstone, the CEO and chairman of Viacom, but was spurned because Redstone believed content was king. Why should he sell MTV or Paramount to AOL? Redstone did not defensively believe that Viacom was an old media company. Levin, who proudly thought he saw around corners, believed Time Warner was old media. He had become almost messianic in his drive to make Time Warner not just bolder but better. He expected it to do good—good deeds, good journalism, to be good for society as well as shareholders. He saw the Internet as the ultimate in his long-held dream to promote interactivity—to push two-way communication, connectivity, community, more choices for more people. In Levin's mind, this was more than a "business" decision. It was a way to advance the public good.

There is another explanation for Levin's evangelicalism: the death of his son. Jonathan Levin, an ebullient, idealistic young man who chose to become a high-school teacher in a tough Bronx neighborhood and befriended his students, was brutally murdered by a former student in 1997. Gerald Levin's friend, Fay Vincent, then (and now) a director of Time Warner, recalled, "I don't think I ever saw a guy so devastated. He couldn't walk at the funeral. It was a defining moment." Levin told Vincent and Dick Parsons he intended to quit. "How can you tell me that growing revenues twenty percent is important?" Levin exclaimed. For the next two months, Levin did not come to the office. Vincent, who was crippled for life as a student at Williams College when he fell from the roof of his dormitory, has some perspective on his friend's turmoil: "For me, everything changed the day I fell off the roof. For Gerry, everything changed on that day. . . . He is a very different person. He's still the same bright guy and has the same character. But his focus is very different."

Indeed. Levin needed to convince himself there would be a larger purpose if he returned to work. Asked about the impact of his son's death, Levin's eyes reddened, and he said, "That's why I'm on a mission. I've obviously been an idealist my whole life, and I guess it always bothered me—I didn't want to be a CEO, I didn't want to be a corporate type. But the way it worked out I was always satisfied to live through my son. What he was doing was the highlight of my life. . . . I thought at the time I wasn't going to return to the company. And then I decided, 'Let's see if

I could make happen through my position some pretty important things, and carry on in that way.' "

Steve Case knew a fair amount about Levin when he phoned him in November of 1999. "I knew he was a believer" in interactivity over the television or the Web, Case recalls. He was also aware that "social issues"—statements of corporate values, pushing something they each called "the public trust" and corporate philanthropy—were important to Levin, as they were to Case. In addition, Case knew what Levin would demand and was prepared to accommodate him. Ken Novack, who had been Case's lawyer and friend and would become vice chairman of the merged companies, remembers war gaming with Case about what was needed to persuade Levin to do a deal: "We believed that the only basis on which Time Warner would be prepared to do a merger with us was if Gerry was the CEO and it was perceived as a merger of equals. That converged with the belief on Steve's part that Gerry would make an excellent CEO."

Personal interests always matter, and the corporate world exemplifies this truism. In an appearance at the 92nd Street Y in the fall of 2000, Levin was interviewed by *Business Week*'s editor-in-chief, Stephen Shepard, and he described the friendly conversations he and Case had had as they traveled to China for a conference the previous fall. Then he described the November phone call: "There's a kind of mating dance, and then there are all these profound questions like who is going to run the company, which shouldn't be the first question, but unfortunately it is." In this initial telephone conversation, Case told Levin that if they could put the companies together, Levin should be CEO and Case would be chairman. "I work better at this sort of strate-gic level," Case remembered telling him.

Case had learned from bitter experience. Back in 1996, when he was the CEO of AOL, the online service was in the throes of its worst crisis. It had recently switched to one flat monthly price for unlimited use, and subscriptions climbed to eight million, but customers got constant busy signals or sudden hang ups. AOL offered refunds, which didn't placate at least thirty-six state attorneys general, who in their capacity as consumer champions launched investigations of the company. Equally troublesome, only nine percent of the company's one billion dollars in revenues came from advertising or merchandising fees. The stock price was in a free fall. Case was dissatisfied with the outside president he had recruited, and asked a member of his board, Robert Pittman, to join the company and restore customer confidence.

Pittman had an unusual background. He had dropped out of college to become a disc jockey in his native Mississippi, and spent the first half of his business career in radio, where he pio-neered the use of audience research. He served as executive pro-ducer of the *Morton Downey Show*, hosted by a loudmouth who often insulted guests. In 1981, he was a co-creator of MTV, and later became CEO of the all-music cable channel. The Pittman-approved slogan, "I want my MTV!" caught on, and Pittman in 1984 was a runner-up to become *Time* magazine's Man of the Year. He would go on to run the Six Flags theme parks, Century 21, a national real estate company, and now AOL.

Case and Pittman were not alike. Case was more an entre-preneur than corporate executive. Case was comfortable talking strategy; Pittman preferred talking about operations. Case would attend Web conferences and enjoyed sharing his dreams about the Internet; Pittman enjoyed talking to Wall Street about how AOL would make its numbers and build a brand. Case talked about the AOL customer; Pittman talked about the AOL shareholder. Case felt awkward in social settings and preferred to stay close to home; Pittman was gregarious and liked the adventure of piloting his plane or rounding up his friends, including *Rolling Stone* founder Jann Wenner and Lehman Brothers managing director Robert Millard, for motorcycle trips around America.

At AOL, Pittman intensely focused on customers, relying on extensive market research and, sometimes, site visits. He never forgot an experience he had had when he was CEO of Six Flags, a financially troubled collection of amusement parks. To see the park from the customer's point of view, he dressed as a janitor. "I learned more in that day about what was going on than perhaps I learned in my whole time there," Pittman once told the *Washington Post*. "Our people who cleaned the park . . . hated our customers because they thought the job was to keep the park clean. Who makes the park dirty? Visitors. We redefined our mission after that. Our job was not about keeping the park clean or about safety; the top priority was about giving the customers the greatest day of their life. . . . Once you tell the street cleaners that's what their job is, they'll be happy to show you where the restroom is."

Pittman and Case succeeded. By 1999, the number of AOL subscribers soared to nearly twenty-five million; revenues climbed from one billion dollars in 1995 to nearly five billion; advertising and commercial income went from nine percent of revenues to over twenty percent; e-commerce sales went from zero to ten billion dollars; AOL's stock was worth fifteen times what it was in 1995; and Steve Case was chairman and made Pittman the CEO.

Case, like Levin, saw a good fit between their companies. This joining of new and old media, each man believed, would be a transforming deal, one that might inject high-voltage energy into both companies. The merger would make AOL Time Warner, as the company would be called, the world's largest media company. By listing the AOL name first, they expected the stock to soar with investors who favored high-growth stocks. And by setting ambitious financial growth goals, they anticipated still other advantages. Powered by the AOL promotional engine, they expected to achieve new synergies. These synergies and the task of meeting ambitious targets, they believed, would erode barriers between the various divisions and instill a new team culture.

After Levin and Case agreed in principle in late 1999 to merge Time Warner and AOL, in December the negotiations almost derailed. Dick Parsons put them back on track. The lawyers and investment bankers and financial officers quibbled over exchange rates and who would get top management posts and serve on the board. A summit meeting was arranged between Case and Levin's chief diplomats, Ken Novack and Dick Parsons. On Christmas Eve, Novack remembered, Parsons got up from his chair and said he was sure they could each go back to their principals and achieve agreement. "Dick has a directness and honesty and a sense of fairness and a sense that a negotiation is not about maximizing but about accommodation," Novack said. "I believe this deal got done because of Dick."

At the wedding announcement, the two companies reversed roles. They called it a merger of equals, but since the smaller new media company had a steeper market valuation, AOL used its inflated stock price to acquire the larger, established media company. And at the January press conference, Levin appeared without his trademark mustache or tie, while Case dressed like Levin once did, in a dark suit and tie. Henceforth, the merged company would have a new dress code. "Gerry took his tie off, and the rest of us did too," said Laurence Kirshbaum, publisher of Time Warner Books. Ted Turner wore a tie to the press conference and was invited to address reporters, telling them of his excitement. He supported the joining of the two companies, he told reporters, "with as much or more excitement and enthusiasm as that first night I made love forty-two years ago!"

Turner was, in fact, angry, but with his personal wealth tied up in the company, he tried to hide this. Levin guessed that the risk of telling Turner and having him sabotage the deal was greater than the risk of not telling his largest shareholder. Besides, the peripatetic Turner was not a part of the core management team. "Ted was not in the loop," a senior executive who is close to Turner said. "Yet Ted did not hesitate to endorse the deal." It was, after all, a growth strategy, and Turner believed in growth. Turner liked that Case was a fellow entrepreneur, not a plodder, and that he too had his personal wealth tied up in the company. Perhaps Case would be a counterweight to Levin, toward whom Turner was feeling estranged. Perhaps Case would support Turner's desire to purchase a broadcast network. Perhaps Case could help bring the Time Warner duchies under central management. Yet at the same time, Turner knew he was not in the room where decisions were being made. According to an AOL strategist who was party to the negotiations, Turner's future role was not even a minor part of these discussions. What was talked about much more, he continued, was what a great fit CNN and AOL would be. "You can AOL-ize CNN and do cross-promotions," the executives said enthusiastically. CNN, in fact, was desperately in need of promotion, for its ratings had plunged and its promotion budget had been cut.

Turner would own about four percent of the new company and remain on the board; he was named a vice chairman, shared the stage when the announcement was made, and graciously accepted the bouquets he received from Levin and Case. But he would not become an integral part of the new management team. While executives at the two companies respected Turner's many successes and his "vision," they also found him unfathomable. One senior AOL executive who was working with Turner for the first time said, "In meetings I've been in with him, he just sits there and in a piercing voice—louder than you would expect someone to talk—he interrupts or conveys a sense of *Hurry up! Why am I here?* He gives off a feeling that he's in a rush, even if he's not doing anything." Although Turner was too proud to say this in the halls of the company he built, he no longer had the desire, or energy, to manage a giant media company. Yet because he was proud, and insulted that his advice was not sought—and worried about his wealth, which was dependent on AOL Time Warner's stock price—his anger simmered just below the surface.

AS USUALLY HAPPENS in a merger, "cultural issues" ensnared the companies in the clumsy initial months of the marriage. "At first the AOL people acted like they acquired us," said one senior Time Warner executive. Some AOL employees swaggered, talking down to their old media counterparts. AOL was a young business whose revenues and profits were exploding; many of Time Warner's divisions were mature businesses. At AOL's corporate headquarters in rural Virginia, the conference rooms were more Spartan and the expense accounts not as lavish as those at Time Warner. Nor did they pay twenty million dollars to entice an actor to star in a movie. AOL's accustomed mode is "ready, fire, aim," said Ken Novack, while Time Warner's mode was more "contemplative." The AOL side was accustomed to announcing ambitious growth targets and meeting them, and Time Warner, which knew its movies might not click that year or that Madonna might be tardy with her latest CD, was more cautious. AOL, said a senior Time Warner executive, "felt the Time Warner folks were too soft and fuzzy." Time Warner executives felt that AOL held them in contempt, as if they were old media dinosaurs.

As the two companies tried to induce their executives to work together to achieve the touted synergies, Turner was largely absent. He was in Atlanta or New York no more than four or five days a month. He was not involved in budget details, as Terry McGuirk was, and so he was not in a position to slow AOL Time

Warner's cost-cutting synergies, including their already announced goal of one billion dollars in savings from combining the two companies. Since McGuirk already ran Turner Broadcasting, the executives reasoned, why engage in a charade? Even McGuirk, an original Turner loyalist, signaled that he "wanted out from under Ted," a senior member of the AOL Time Warner team explained. McGuirk admired Turner, but if McGuirk was to be held responsible, then he wanted the authority too.

There was one other difficulty. In the reorganized company, Steve Case was going to be the chairman and Levin the CEO, and the idea was to divide the company into separate spheres, each reporting to one of two presidents. Time Warner's Dick Parsons would oversee movies, music, publishing, legal affairs, and human resources. AOL's Robert Pittman would oversee AOL, cable, the magazines, television (including HBO, Turner Broadcasting, and the Warner Bros. television network), and business development. "It made no sense for Ted to report to Bob," a senior AOL Time Warner strategist said. "Just as it would make little sense for Bob to be in charge and yet to have Ted report to Gerry. If you did that, how would Bob do his job? By a process of elimination, it made sense for Terry McGuirk to report to Bob and for Ted to take a strategic role."

Sometimes Turner made light of his diminished role. Lou Dobbs remembered being invited to Turner's Montana ranch for a weekend. The relationship between these two men went way back to 1980 when Turner hired Dobbs at CNN, and they became friends when Dobbs served on Turner Broadcasting's Executive Committee before he left in 1999 to start an Internet venture, Space.com; Dobbs returned in early 2001 to, among other things, anchor his old show *Moneyline*. As the two friends were fishing, Dobbs said, "Ted, I outrank you. I'm CEO and chairman."

"You're forgetting," Turner said. "I'm also chairman of the Turner Foundation."

"Ted, that's nonprofit!"

"What do you think Space.com is?" Turner retorted, laughing.

Dobbs laughed too when telling this story, but like many of Turner's friends, he was angry. "He has not been treated with the respect due him," Dobbs said.

Surely Turner did not feel he was treated properly when CNN canceled a pet project of his—a multipart documentary exploring the proliferation of nuclear weapons. In 1999, Turner had watched producer George Crile's stunning hour on CBS's *60 Minutes II*, which for the first time took viewers inside the Russian nuclear command bunker. Turner turned his charm on Crile, and although he could not lure him away from CBS, he did get him to agree to report, write, and produce a CNN documentary—the model would be CNN's twenty-four-hour *Cold War* series, said Turner. Soon after Crile started work, Turner told him that he was encountering budget opposition at CNN. They would have to scale the project back to three hours. By October of 2000, it was down to a single hour. "There's a lot of pressure to make the budgets," Turner explained, disappointed. Turner, in fact, was so agitated by the budgeting strictures at CNN that he told me, "I am going to produce, myself, ten hours on nuclear proliferation and chemical and biological warfare. I'll give first crack to CNN, and if they don't want it, I'll give it to PBS." (By the spring of 2001, CNN's founder had given up on CNN documentaries. Together with former associates like Pat Mitchell, who is the president of PBS, and Robert Wussler, who had been a top Turner Broadcasting executive, he planned to team up with correspondent Bill Moyers for a series of PBS documentaries on world issues; the Turner Foundation was to provide half the financing. "Over the next few years I would hope we would do one hundred hours," Wussler said.)

"I always wanted CNN to be the *New York Times* of television," Turner said. Now, he fretted, that goal was more distant. And he knew the reason: "For the last four years we were asked to grow twenty-percent-a-year compounded profits for our division [Turner Broadcasting]. We've done it." Turner had misgivings about the goal, but said "it was a reality." He's a team player, and the team game, said CNN chairman Tom Johnson, is that today "there is much less enthusiasm for high-cost, low-audience long-form documentaries that were near and dear to Ted's heart." In the past, many of these documentaries lost money, he said, but CNN did them anyway "because Ted wanted us to do them. Most of them are terrific." When he slashed the Crile project from three hours to one, Johnson said, "Ted wasn't happy. I don't think he's happy with me. Ted knows I'm in a new world today." Turner was reminded of this "new world" when he invited me to sit in on a CNN Executive Committee meeting on December 19, 2000, and the invitation was rescinded. "He invited you to a meeting that is not his meeting," an AOL Time Warner executive explained.

Then, in January of 2001, although Turner called CNN "the most profitable news operation in the world"—it earned three hundred million dollars the previous year—its staff of more than four thousand was reduced by nearly ten percent. CNN was so much more profitable partly because it had few highly paid "stars," it had no union wages and work rules, and it did not air highly polished, expensively produced programs. Nevertheless, to meet its profit goals, CNN was ordered to slash its overhead. Those who were invited to leave included such Turner stalwarts as Barbara Pyle, Nick Charles, Elsa Klensch, Gene Randall, and the Atlanta-based Turner Environmental Division, with its show, *People Count*, which Fonda sometimes hosted. On CNN evening programs, talk replaced news reports—often with the shouting-head format that CNN inaugurated with *Crossfire* and which Fox News and MSNBC had copied and extended. Neither Fox nor MSNBC cover the world, observed the former CNN/U.S. president Rick Kaplan. "Basically, the Fox prime-time schedule is just talk radio. . . . And with the networks convinced they don't need to cover the world, there really is a need for CNN. You need to have one network that really covers the news, not talks about covering the news."

The concern expressed by Kaplan was shared within CNN. Christiane Amanpour, CNN's star overseas correspondent, said, "Ted Turner . . . believes in the value of news and information, and believes in it as a public service. That's what I'm waiting to see: If his successors do too." CNN chairman Tom Johnson was worried as well. He talked to CEO Levin, who reassured him that *Time* magazine and CNN were the "two crown jewels in the company." Johnson also said that Bob Pittman assured him that he and his colleagues in New York believed in CNN's mission. But Pittman's definition of CNN's mission may not have matched Johnson's or Turner's.

It was easy for Pittman to say he believed in CNN and news. But he also believed in maximizing profit margins and the stock price. He had no background in news and therefore might not appreciate how daily journalism is an inherently wasteful process: it involves waiting for calls to be returned, for airlines to fly, keeping forty-two international and domestic bureaus functioning, chasing stories that don't pan out, and sometimes working for days on a single story. Would stockholders think this productive? Would Pittman?

As late as December of 2000, a longtime Turner Broadcasting executive predicted, "Ted will protect us." Yet by March of 2001, Turner's business influence was diminished further when the parent company announced that his top lieutenants at Turner Broadcasting, Terence McGuirk, the chairman and CEO, and Steven J. Heyer, the president, would be replaced by Jamie Kellner, the chief executive and founder of the Warner Bros. broadcast network. To achieve more of the company's much-touted synergies, Turner Broadcasting would be folded into a combined broadcast-and-cable-television division, which would be run by Kellner, who would move to Atlanta from Hollywood. In a press release, Turner applauded Kellner's promotion. He was pleased that the separate fiefdoms in his old company and Time Warner would be joined. He blamed Levin for wanting "to keep everyone weak so he could be stronger." But he was sorry that AOL Time

Warner was practicing what he thinks of as management by the numbers, and he knew that he wouldn't feel as free to barge into Kellner's office as he did McGuirk's or Heyer's.

Turner also knew that McGuirk and Heyer chafed at AOL Time Warner's demand that Turner Broadcasting's "operating profits" (which are earnings before interest, taxes, depreciation, and amortization are subtracted, or EBITDA) grow by thirty-nine percent in 200, which Turner said was nearly double the actual profit-growth average of the company over the past five years. The divisions that traditionally grew more slowly, like music and books, were allowed lower growth targets, while faster-growing divisions, like Turner Broadcasting and AOL, were taxed with more ambitious targets. The growth target for the entire company in 2001 was thirty percent. Of Turner Broadcasting executives, Ted Turner said, "They were unhappy because the financial goals they were given were unreachable without hurting the company."

AOL Time Warner executives insisted that the true profit-growth target for the Turner Broadcasting division was half what Turner claimed, and that his thirty-nine percent did not reflect significant accounting changes. (Nonsense, senior executives at Turner Broadcasting retorted, claiming that their operating profits in 2000 were just under a billion dollars and that their company-imposed goal for 2001 was nearly $1.4 billion.) AOL Time Warner executives also said they wanted McGuirk to stay but that he graciously stepped aside rather than endure new turmoil; they insisted that Heyer was not deterred by this and actually sought the top job but was spurned by Pittman, who decided to bring in Jamie Kellner instead. While Pittman wouldn't talk about these management changes, associates said he was disturbed that CNN had lost market share to Fox News and even to third-place MSNBC. CNN's prime-time ratings were dropping. CNN's programming, Pittman believed, was stale. Ted Turner did not disagree that CNN needed to be spruced up, but he was much more worried about Fox News, which was available in fewer homes but was now reaching a larger audience than CNN.

Where Turner and Pittman disagreed was over what Turner believed were arbitrary budget goals for CNN—what he called the company's new preoccupation with "short-term fluctuations" in its stock price. "I never ran the company by the numbers," Turner said. Pittman denied that the company was being run strictly by the numbers. "I agree with Ted: there is no number that is worth it to screw up a franchise." But, he added, "everyone agreed on" a growth target number including, he implied, McGuirk and Heyer. Asked about the growth target, McGuirk refused to comment. He did say, "The numbers are given to us, not negotiated." The issue at CNN was the same bottom-line question highlighted by the early 2001 resignation from Knight Ridder of Jay T. Harris, publisher of the *San Jose Mercury News*: Is there a point at which the corporate demand for ever steeper profit margins does violence to good journalism?

Wall Street was not happy with AOL Time Warner's second-quarter numbers in 2001, but Ted Turner and journalists at the company had even more reason to be unhappy. To meet its profit-growth targets, the company speeded its cost cutting. Time Inc. offered buyouts to more than five hundred editorial employees who were fifty years or older and had been with the company at least fifteen years. Some experienced correspondents—New York–based Ed Barnes, who had covered six wars for *Time* magazine, and Bill Dowell, who had been all over the world—were lopped from the payroll. The Time Inc. research library was closed, eliminating three-dozen employees. A layer of copy editors was shaved, following a cut a few years earlier of researchers. Now that three layers had been pared in the past decade—researchers, copy editors, and librarians—a senior *Time* writer worried, "There is no one to catch the reporters" and to correct facts. Editors won't catch errors "because they're dealing with a dozen stories a week. And remember, these stories come in Friday night when everyone is exhausted." Some bureaus were already stretched thin. *Time*, for example, covered Europe with two correspondents and two stringers based in Paris (along with a researcher), and with junior stringers in other capitals. Not that a full array of international news appears in *Time*—or the other newsweeklies—anymore.

Daniel Okrent, who in his career at Time Inc. had been the managing editor of *Life* and the editor of the New Media division, was one of the senior writers who chose to accept the buyout. Okrent was well regarded by his bosses, but at fifty-three, he wanted to write a book and spend time with his family on the Cape. He praised Time Inc. president Don Logan and Time Inc. editor-in-chief Norman Pearlstein as defenders of "quality journalism," and said "a lot of good journalism" is done by *Time* because *People Magazine* throws off $350 million in profits. Yet he thought the changes at Time Inc. were momentous: "This is changing the culture, I believe, in radical ways. Some of them are positive"—the buyouts meant that younger people would be promoted earlier, for instance. But he wondered: Would the best people flee? Since "good journalism is expensive," would quality suffer? He mentioned the recent firing of *Time* correspondent Ed Barnes. "The real story," Okrent said, "is that the kind of journalism that Ed chases is not valued anymore. . . . Maybe we killed Ed yesterday, but we disabled him several years ago when we decided as editors that the kind of stories Ed Barnes did was no longer at the center of our journalistic ambition." He conceded, "Readers don't want to read it," but said editors must sometimes be willing to defy the audience or pay a price: "You miss the surprises if you're not willing to make investments. . . . What I fear is that Time Inc. will become just another company. It's not special anymore."

Even CNN, which had been noted for its international coverage, had curbed international news. In July of 2001, when China was selected to host the 2008 Olympics, the story received scant coverage on CNN. This would, no doubt, upset Levin, who wore a tie when he announced in June that the company was partnering with China's largest computer maker to develop interactive services for China, and who believed the American press was too negative about China. "I have great respect for the Chinese government and what they're trying to do there after one hundred years of being run over by other countries," he said. While CNN advertises that it has twice the number of overseas bureaus as CBS, NBC, and ABC combined, many of these bureaus are manned by junior staffers. "More than fifty percent of our over-

seas coverage is now supplied by news services, not CNN,"
complained an overseas correspondent. Increasingly, this correspondent said, senior editors at CNN "equate serious with boring."
Senior executives at CNN, as at the other cable and broadcast
networks that have more dramatically shrunk international coverage, asserted that there was no big news overseas. They were
not saying, nothing important is happening overseas. They were
really saying that in order to get ratings, we need wars or some
kind of crisis.

They made do with Chandra Levy—just as they made do with
O. J. Simpson when the network reported to Ted Turner.
Throughout much of July in 2001, for example, Larry King
devoted the vast majority of his programs to the case of the
missing Washington intern and her congressman-paramour. The
Chandra Levy/Gary Condit story was featured on Larry King on
six of seven nights in late August, and more nights than not was
the centerpiece of most of CNN's prime-time programs.

Asked about quality and journalism, senior executives at the
company said the correct thing. "I'm absolutely committed in my
soul to investing in news," said Levin. But the company was not
investing in news. Although he tried to be a good team player by
keeping silent, Ted Turner was vexed. The man who started out
in television disdainful of news had become a believer. As he
became more of an internationalist, more of a questioner of the
accepted wisdom, Turner embraced the vital role that news
played in a democracy. He also had a grandiose vision of his own
role. "I'm going to do the news like the world has never seen

news before," he said at the time. "This will be the most significant achievement in the annals of journalism."

Gerald Levin also cared about journalism, but when he spoke of "quality" or "trust," it wasn't clear that he truly comprehended what the words meant. Would he back an expensive documentary series on the Cold War, as Turner had? Turner had had his own lapses when CNN and Turner Broadcasting still reported to him, but he understood that some things couldn't be quantified. It is easy to quantify the number of journalists in a company, or the number of overseas bureaus. It is far more difficult for businessmen to quantify the quality of the journalism or whether it engenders trust. If fewer reporters have less time to report stories, therefore rushing them, and don't have a rigorous system to check facts, this may not produce journalism worthy of trust. There are terrific journalists at Time Inc. and CNN who get up each day determined to fulfill their public trust, to get the facts right and to be fair. The burgeoning concern among many journalists at the company was that the support system did not always cooperate to advance that goal. Ted Turner underpaid his employees and skimped on costs, but his journalists believed that he would open his wallet and back them to cover important news. CNN employees did not extend that trust to his successors—with reason, since they seemed to care more about the brand than the journalism. "Part of my goal is to create excitement for the CNN brand," Jamie Kellner told me in explaining what he saw as the foremost challenge confronting CNN. He said he wanted to make CNN look less "stodgy," to not only attract more "eyeballs" but also keep "them a longer period of time," and he hoped to appeal to younger viewers. These, of course, are business, not journalistic challenges, and it is a novel form of convergence that the men running AOL Time Warner often conflated the two. Of course, as businessmen they were aliens to journalists, just as, to them, journalists were from another planet.

TED TURNER WAS getting more notice outside his company than in it. When Fidel Castro came to New York in 2000 for a three-day summit meeting at the UN, he wanted to spend one night having dinner with Turner, who flew in from Montana for the occasion. Castro had not only hunted with Turner, he remembered that CNN was the first American news network to open a bureau in Havana, one of thirty-seven bureaus it now maintained overseas. Turner was the first Western businessman to have a private audience with Russia's new president, Vladimir Putin, who, Turner remembers, used to drive him when Turner visited St. Petersburg and Putin was a deputy to the city's mayor. "I learned the value of being nice to everyone!" Turner joked. In a trip arranged by George Crile, in May of 2000 Turner visited a nuclear command center outside Moscow. General Vladimir Yakovlev, the commander of Russia's Strategic Rocket Forces, sat Turner in his chair in a small, rectangular room and cautioned, "Don't touch any buttons!" There was a PowerPoint presentation in English, delineating Russia's various nuclear forces. Turner learned that each of the then-seven-thousand warheads could obliterate everything within a one- to two-mile radius before the radiation and the fires spread. Turner sat mute, Eason Jordan recalls, for an hour and a half, transfixed by what he heard and saw. "It was the only time I ever saw him speechless," said Jordan. Turner could not take his eye off the Russian saints that hung from the wall of what was once godless communism's command center.

A dark cloud hung over Turner. He feared a nuclear conflagration was imminent, that it would likely be triggered by some colossal human error, and this personal nightmare propelled him to feel he must do more. He traveled incessantly, speaking of the good that would come if only humans were kinder, more trusting. A man who didn't trust business competitors was asking governments to trust each other. It was terribly naïve, but also terribly endearing. He spoke as a citizen of the world, not as an American. He put his money where his mouth was in support of the UN. He opposed a bipolar, balance-of-power world, preferring a UN where all nations had a voice. He became the champion of the dispossessed. And he was a bona fide celebrity—Captain Courageous, Mr. CNN, Mr. Billionaire, Mr. Fonda.

People and government leaders around the world watched CNN. "The Carter Center has programs in sixty-five nations," Jimmy Carter said. "We deal with leaders of nations who have a human-rights problem or conflict. . . . We go to those countries, and they quite often do not have a U.S. embassy in them. Invariably, in the offices there will be a TV station tuned to CNN." They know about Turner, and they know, Carter added, that Turner is a true citizen of the world, a man who speaks up for what he believes even when it offends his government. Carter described Turner as a personal "hero." Kofi Annan sees this in Turner's appeal. "He and Castro have a similar quality," Annan said. "They are folk heroes of a sort. You can have one hundred heads of state here, and most people will gravitate toward Castro. You can have one hundred media heads here, and people will gravitate toward Ted."

"He has leverage because of who he is," NBC's Bob Wright observed. "If he wants to get a message out, the world press will deliver it." As long as the press gravitates to Turner, he will retain some leverage over his company.

He surely maintains some leverage over college students, as a two-day visit to Harvard in March of 2001 demonstrated. An evening appearance at the Kennedy School of Government drew a large audience. Turner was introduced by Alex S. Jones, the director of the Joan Shorenstein Center on the Press, Politics and Public Policy, who said Turner was a southerner who more resembled Elvis Presley than Robert E. Lee. As Elvis single-handedly changed American music, said Jones, "Ted Turner changed America" with his invention of CNN. Turner jumped up on the low platform and, without looking at him, pumped Jones's hand and started talking, with Jones still at his side. Turner used no notes. He wore the same blue corduroy jacket and gray slacks he wore all week. Perhaps it was the way he jumped up and, in his joltingly loud voice, started talking quickly, or the way he suddenly paused and drawled, "Ahhhhhhhhhhhhh"; or perhaps it was the way he seemed to lapse into self-pity when he said, "I'm just trying to do the best I can," or the way he raced from subject to subject, sometimes letting thoughts collide—how he was rejected by Harvard when he applied, and how he'd given Jane Fonda a hundred million dollars, and how, just recently, she bestowed more than twelve million of that sum on Harvard's School of Education for the study of gender and education, how he wasn't a journalist but had related to the species since he sold newspapers as a boy—perhaps it was these quirks that caused the audience, as often happens when Turner speaks, to giggle. "I thought he was drunk when he stood up," said Michael Baumgartner, a first-year graduate student at the Kennedy School. Watching Turner speak is like watching live TV, with the audience wondering what will happen next.

But although at first people seemed to be laughing at Turner, the feeling in the room soon changed. On being told that President Bush earlier that day had abandoned a campaign pledge to establish for the first time under the Clean Air Act "mandatory reduction targets" for carbon-dioxide emissions by power plants, Turner was momentarily silenced. "That's heartbreaking news," he said finally. "I mean, I can't take any more bad news. I've lost my job and my wife!" Turner went on to talk about the environment, and about curbing nuclear weapons, and about his commitment to news. This was not a typical Kennedy School talk, which tends to be more formal and serious. When he finished, students clamored to shake his hand. One master's degree candidate, Cynthia Hogle, said she was taken by his sense of humor, which made him "approachable and human." Instead of being bothered by his considerable "ego," which was her overwhelming first impression, as Turner spoke she said she was impressed by his candor and vulnerability, which added up to an impression that Turner was "genuine."

That night, Turner was discreet about CNN. Asked about its future, he said, "Well, I hope it's a bright one." But by the next morning, the man who confesses to a congenital inability to police a secret was no longer restrained. Turner was featured in a roundtable discussion moderated by Jones, and although he did not plan to betray his anger, before an audience of about 150 members of the Harvard community he could not contain it. Out flowed his distress with the management of AOL Time Warner. While Turner did not criticize the recent round of cutbacks at CNN, he did criticize the parent company's decision to impose on Turner Broadcasting in the coming year what he said was an operating profit-growth target of thirty-nine percent. This was impossible to achieve, Turner said, without doing harm to CNN's journalism, especially since half of CNN's revenues come from advertising and the ad marketplace was collapsing. The consequences would be unintended but real, he said, and would occur because "the incredible emphasis on making the numbers each quarter makes the management more worried about making the numbers than about the journalism." When he ran CNN and war broke out in Kosovo or Baghdad, he said, "We put the journalism first. They're saying they will put the journalism first, but they can't." Since CNN would make approximately $325 million this year, he suggested that the parent company should unglue itself from a preoccupation with Wall Street and think more about the long-term harm they might do to the valuable CNN brand.

Turner worried about CNN's future. He worried because CNN's ratings had fallen by 5 percent over the previous twelve months, while Fox's climbed by 132 percent and MSNBC's by 51 percent. He knew that CNN now faced twenty-four-hour competitors that didn't exist when CNN started—Fox News, MSNBC, CNBC, and regional and local cable news outlets that already outdraw CNN in their localities, plus the Internet. He worried in particular about the Fox network, which has conservative talk-show hosts like Bill O'Reilly, now reaching a larger audience than Larry King, CNN's ratings champ. Turner blamed Murdoch for deliberately exciting a conservative viewer base, yet CNN's answer to this challenge seemed to be to copy Fox by moving away from its traditional credo (news is the star) and away from documentaries and instead introducing more (and cheaper) talk and, consequently, less reporting.

While insisting that "we are still going to do news here," Tom Johnson nevertheless admitted, "Fox has really been making big gains on us with talk shows. We have to be willing to change." Before he exited as Turner Broadcasting's number two executive, eventually becoming the chief operating officer for Coca-Cola, Steve Heyer had ideas as to how CNN could change. The former management consultant who occupied Ted Turner's old office on the third floor of the Techwood Drive headquarters of Turner Broadcasting told me his vision was for CNN to do more news viewers could use. He pulled out a storyboard with a model ad campaign entitled, "Why does Bosnia matter to you?" Heyer explained, "So what do I want the programming of CNN to look like? I told them I'd like a show, *Why Should I Care?* Have Jeff

Greenfield take three issues that day and show how they affect my life." He also envisioned a show, which he thought novel, that would be called *Winners and Losers*. It would, he said, delineate "who's up and who's down, and why? That may give another edge to the show." Who's in and who's out, of course, is not new. And such ridiculous chit-chat is cheaper to produce, and helps meet ever escalating budget targets.

Perhaps nothing will reverse CNN's slow ratings slide. As happened to ABC, CBS, and NBC, CNN is experiencing the audience erosion that comes with competition. With competition from cable news and the Internet, the danger was that CNN's news was becoming a commodity. While Turner thought CNN had programmed "too much" talk, he confessed that he had no idea how to cure its ratings woes: "Quite frankly, I'm not sure I have the answers of what to do." Privately, however, he is concerned about a general dumbing down that is taking place in the media, putting "DiSiprio"—he means Leonardo DiCaprio—"on the cover of *Time*. Obviously, it should be on the cover of *People* or *Entertainment Weekly!*"

8

Hubris

Ted Turner's goal in merging with Time Warner in 1995 was the same goal Time Warner had when it sold itself to AOL in 2000: beliefs that size conferred advantages, that corporate synergies would be found, and magically, that one plus one would equal three. Company leaders believed that by cross-promoting each other, the record division could sell more CDs over AOL, AOL could lure more subscribers through Time Warner Cable, and Time Warner books could be made into Warner Bros. movies. With a faith as deep as a religious fundamentalist's, Gerald Levin and Steve Case and their compatriots believed the disparate interests of each division could be harmonized. They believed everyone would sacrifice a division for a corporate goal.

The company was organized to produce success, and by the spring of 2001 there had been some successes. Twice a month, the divisional CEOs and executive staff of AOL Time Warner gathered in a conference room on the thirty-fourth floor of the

Time Life Building at Rockefeller Center for a marathon meeting that sometimes included lunch. A seat at one end of the
twenty-two-foot-long mahogany table was reserved for Levin; it
was unoccupied even when he was away. No seat was reserved
for Turner, who was not invited. Opposite Levin, at the other end
of the table, sat the two co-chief operating officers of the company, Robert Pittman and Richard Parsons. Eleven divisional
CEOs and ten other senior executives, including one woman, sat
in leather swivel chairs on either side of the seven-foot-wide
table. The meetings lasted for three to four hours, and no one
worried about speaking too softly, for a voice-amplification system was built into the table. Noises from outside were muted by
a gray fabric covering the walls. Motorized shades slid down if
too much sun streamed through the windows facing west to the
Hudson River. Having abandoned neckties around the time AOL
and Time Warner announced their merger in January of 2000,
most of the male executives wore the new-media uniform of
open-necked shirts and no jackets. Few looked casual, however,
since suit pants and dress shirts buttoned tightly at the sleeves
comprised the norm.

No one affected a more casual look than Levin, the sixty-two-
year-old who ruled over the world's largest and most powerful
media company. No other communications colossus touched as
many consumers. None owned as many pieces of the food chain
as did AOL Time Warner—from the publishing companies that
create the initial idea, to the Hollywood factories that produce it,
to the networks that air it, to the cable systems or online engine
that deliver and ensure its promotion. AOL Time Warner was as

close to being vertically integrated as any company. The Internet? AOL was the gateway half of all Americans use to access the Internet, delivering twice as much mail as the U.S. Postal Service, and its Netscape software division made Web browsers and other computer applications. Print? With more than 130 titles, including *Time, People, Fortune,* and *Sports Illustrated,* AOL Time Warner was the world's largest magazine publisher, selling one-fourth of all consumer magazine advertising—more ads than the next three magazine groups combined. Cable? With thirteen million subscribers, Time Warner Cable reached about twenty percent of all cable homes and was the nation's second-largest cable company; its broadband business, Road Runner, used its thick cable pipe to provide more high-speed access to the Internet than any competitor. Movies? Warner Bros. was one of the seven major movie studios, with a library of seven thousand feature films, and its New Line Cinema would deliver such huge hits as *Lord of the Rings.* Television? Warner Bros. supplied more programming to the television networks and stations than any studio, including its own WB network, and its library contained thirty-two thousand TV programs and thirteen thousand animated features; and Turner Broadcasting, which owns four of the top-ten cable networks (TNT, TBS, the Cartoon Network, and CNN), generated more revenues than any cable network, and CNN reached about one billion viewers around the world. Pay television? With thirty-seven million subscribers, HBO ranked number one, and with hits like *The Sopranos* and *Sex and the City,* it sprinted ahead of competitors. Music? The Warner Music Group was one of five music behemoths, owning more than one million music copyrights. E-commerce? In 2000, AOL members spent twenty billion dollars buying goods online, double the previous year's total. In all, the company counted 137 million subscribers—twice the combined total of its two nearest non–telephone company competitors, News Corp and Vivendi— and each month its products were sampled by an estimated 2.5 billion consumers. If Levin and Case succeeded in their "mission" to make AOL Time Warner "the premier growth company" and "the most valued company in the world"—worth more than Exxon, General Electric, or General Motors—it would become a global superpower, richer than Microsoft.

To achieve this mission, Levin told Wall Street analysts in July, "We're running the company through the financial function." Levin, as this statement to analysts suggests, spoke differently to Wall Street than he did to the press. He dropped talk of his social mission, of spending whatever it took to improve CNN or *Time*. Instead he emphasized his unwillingness to allow anything to intrude on his quest to bolster the bottom line.

Although he often derided short-term Wall Street thinking, Levin, who dressed down with a vengeance in pale green khakis, flap-pocket shirts, and scuffed, thick-soled work shoes, pleaded guilty to having adopted a new persona. "I'm a hawk on margins," he told me. When the merger was approved, AOL Time Warner turned its attention to Wall Street. In January 2001, the top officers of the new company orchestrated an Investor Day. Each CEO made a presentation complete with charts and expressions of buoyant optimism. A thick binder of the presentations was handed to each guest. The words and charts were crafted to appeal to Wall Street investors searching for the magic words *cost savings* and *growth*. Forget talk of a downturn in advertising, Levin said when he followed Case. With the fervor of a true believer, Levin said his company was "in a different zone"; it was not just another media company that sold ads in familiar ways. It could use "the AOL machine" to sell its magazines, its music, movies, television, cable, and books.

Levin's principal agent in meeting the company's growth targets was Bob Pittman, whose management style was crisp and to the point, leaving little time for chat. With his self-assured announcer's voice, at meetings Pittman often entered sales-speak mode, extolling AOL Time Warner's "branded products" and "three subscription machines," noting that "nothing stands in our way of using our cross-company assets" and our weekly reviews of "actionable metrics" and our "multiple ways to monetize" consumer relationships. Pittman had a single-minded focus: achieving the numbers the company promised.

For the year 2001, the company set ambitious goals—a thirty percent rise in EBITDA; in all, management expected earnings of eleven billion dollars, profit margins of thirty percent, and revenues that would top forty billion dollars. The company monitored these targets at the biweekly CEO meeting, whose agenda was shaped by Pittman. Each Friday, then chief financial officer J. Michael Kelly sent to attendees a report on each division's performance to date for the quarter—ad revenues, new subscribers, e-commerce revenues, sales figures—versus the budget projections. To induce the executives to look up from their small personal digital assistants, which wirelessly tether them to their office and e-mail, at the start of each CEO meeting Kelly reviewed what was referred to as "key metrics by division." If the division was falling below targets, he asked, "What are you going to do to get where we want to be?" The reason for the aggressive growth targets, said Kelly, a trained accountant who spent much of his career in the telephone industry, was Wall Street: it didn't "understand AOL Time Warner. What's a comparable company? There is none." No other company bridges new media and old, no other company includes so many diverse media businesses. "We still have two analysts at each Wall Street firm analyzing us, not one." He continued, "It was felt that we needed to put some financial goals out there so people could get their heads around us. It was a way of filling in the education process as we go along." It was the same technique Jack Welch employed in 1981, when he assumed the chairmanship of the conglomerate General Electric. By announcing ambitious revenue and profit margin targets, executives must strive each quarter to climb an imposing hill.

Chairman Case believed that another reason to set such ambitious financial goals was to cleanse the old Time Warner culture. "A critique of the old Time Warner was that it was run almost as a holding company," Case told me. "To some extent, this was true. It was a way to attract and keep strong managers who would each manage businesses independently. That was then. This is now. The markets are blurring and the technologies are converging and now it is best to integrate the businesses. Now it's about building bridges and driving synergies, and these require a new culture that focuses on meeting the consumer's needs." To meet

the publicly stated numerical targets "forces cooperation," he
said, before adding, "Do I worry that short-term concerns about
the numbers will retard investments? Yes. But at this stage, the
benefits outweigh the risks."

But not everyone was on board. Certainly not Ted Turner. And
although he always behaved like the superb team player that he
was, privately Dick Parsons, then fifty-two, echoed Turner's concerns. Parsons voiced a skepticism secretly shared by others
within the executive ranks of the old Time Warner. When I asked
if the company was placing too much emphasis on its Wall Street
audience, the avuncular Parsons answered, "Yes. This is a tension
that as managers we have to deal with. We're not a quarter horse.
I read somewhere that the quarter horse is the fastest animal in
the world in a quarter of a mile. Because of lots of dynamics,
increasingly the marketplace is demanding quarter by quarter
performance that has the potential to undermine the long term."
To build for the long term, he continued, the company must
invest to expand overseas, investments that might take five years
to succeed. He said he did not disagree with the need to push
everyone to meet aggressive targets. But since his responsibilities
were mostly on the content side of the business—movies,
records, books—"I worry about it somewhat more than my colleagues. The content side is still a hit-driven business. If you're
AOL or cable, you start the year with twenty-eight million subs
[subscribers] or thirteen million subs, and you can plan your
growth. You've got a base. But if you're Warner Bros. or Warner
Music, every year you start with the till empty." Predictions are
guesses.

To grow by nearly a third each year requires more than cost cutting, though the company did an immodest amount of this. Since January of 2001, it had sliced about eight thousand jobs. To succeed, AOL Time Warner needed to invent new businesses, or new ways of managing old businesses, which is where the twin gods worshipped at the new company—synergy and convergence—were joined. This is why the biweekly CEO meeting included discussions on synergy and teamwork. The idea was for each division of the company to become, in part, a promotional and sales vehicle for the others. They would advertise *Harry Potter* T-shirts on AOL, then sell them at the AOL online store. They would combine television, print, and cable into a single sales package to be sold to advertisers. Magazine subscriptions were sold on AOL's opening screen. Madonna CDs were hawked through AOL contests and through a *People* feature story that became a CNN special. More AOL sign-up discs were included in Time Inc.'s numerous publications. Because the new AOL Time Warner owned both distribution channels (cable, a TV network, AOL) and content (magazines, music, movies, television, books), it had what Levin described to Wall Street analysts as "leverage points"—sway over advertisers, artists, producers, competitors, and consumers.

The unspoken assumption of leverage—this new business arithmetic—is that one plus one equals more than two because the whole equals more than the parts. This is where convergence entered their thinking. "If I look at AOL today at twenty-four dollars per household," Barry Schuler, then the CEO of AOL, breathlessly said, "ten years from now that could be seventy or one hundred dollars, when you think that you won't have to buy CDs or rent from the video store or go to the telephone company and AOL will service your wireless devices." AOL Time Warner hoped in that way to become the Wal-Mart of the Information Age, a one-stop-shopping company.

AOL Time Warner expected to mine money from various sources: selling subscriptions; selling advertising; selling individual products like music, movies, TV programs, books, and T-shirts; selling services like AOLTV that fuses the TV and the personal computer; selling telephone service over the cable wire; selling software from its Netscape subsidiary; selling marketing agreements that provide advertisers with access to consumers' shopping lists; snatching a piece of the e-commerce done over AOL; renting real estate space on the AOL mall to other companies or on their broadband cable wire to other Internet service providers; or selling to other companies the same promotional trampoline AOL provided its own divisions. Compared to broadcast television, which relied only on advertising revenues, or to print, which generated revenues from advertising and circulation, AOL Time Warner hoped to feast on multiple revenue streams. "This is not a media company anymore; it's not an Internet company," Levin almost giddily boasted to investors in January of 2001. "It truly is a one-of-a-kind company. . . ."

A sister of synergy, of course, is shilling. To ensure synergy, after the biweekly CEO meeting, Pittman's deputy, Mayo Stuntz, e-mailed to each participant a lengthy review of the "cross-divisional initiatives" they agreed to undertake and the status of each. For example, one three-page, single-spaced Stuntz memorandum to all members of the CEO meeting outlined cross-divisional initiatives, and under the entry for Madonna's tour Stuntz reported what other divisions were doing, including supposedly independent CNN, which was planning a summer TV special in concert with a *People Magazine* feature on the singer.

One synergy home run came when the WB television network launched the show *Popstars*, in which young women competed to form a new pop group. At one CEO meeting, Roger Ames, CEO of the music group, offered to award a Warner Music contract to the winner, and AOL's Schuler promised to create "buzz" by featuring the program on the AOL welcome screen and in ads that asked the audience to come up with a name for the group; Don Logan, head of the magazine group, offered a full-page ad and a sweepstakes contest in *Entertainment Weekly*, plus promotions on Time Inc. Web sites. The numbers were impressive: the CD of the new band, called Eden's Crush, debuted at No. 6 on *Billboard*'s chart of the top two hundred; and its single, "Get Over Yourself," was the No. 1 single in America. "They became a phenomenon," Parsons said. "A manufactured phenomenon."

For Aurora Wallace, an instructor in New York University's Department of Culture and Communications, the company's constant cross-promotion and selling "empties content of anything but a consumption message. If every part of the company has to serve every other part of the company, there's no incentive to talk about anything else," she said. "It's not evil. It's logical, according to corporate logic. The problem is that we expect the media to do other things. To inform us. To provide social glue. If that glue is only about consumption, we are missing something. It creates a grand illusion of choice."

To have listened to company executives piously speak of their public trust obligations, one would think that what was good for AOL Time Warner was always synonymous with the public good. Of course, it was not. When AOL features on its opening screen an array of offerings from sister companies, as Aurora Wallace suggested, it is selling merchandise under the guise of offering consumers more choice. Jeffrey Chester, executive director of the consumer-oriented Center for Digital Democracy, said, "What a company like AOL Time Warner wants is to control the consumer or customer." He believed that what the company promotes as more consumer choice may become a walled garden that traps consumers on AOL's planet rather than allowing them easy and open access to the Internet universe. Microsoft's MSN subscribers, as an instance, don't have access to AOL's dominant Instant Messaging. Was this because of security concerns, as AOL insisted, or because AOL wanted to cripple a competitor? Managing the company by the numbers may be good for the stock price, but it also may starve its journalism. And corporate size may enhance a company's leverage and global reach, at the same time diminishing the localism and community ties that matter more to citizens than to shareholders.

If cable became the broadband pipe providing access to the Internet and to the new medium that interactive television would become, if it became the means to plug all appliances into a single network, then a manipulative gatekeeper was a menace.

"AOL Time Warner will be like an air controller, deciding who gets landing rights and who gets gates," said Chester, one of many consumer advocates who had urged the government to challenge the merger of AOL and Time Warner. "They can make sure that their services and content get preferential treatment. They are going to give themselves the fastest speed." The new company could detour upstart competitors by charging steep access fees. In the same way that cable systems have granted coveted lower-numbered channel positions to networks they own or that pay more, so those who controlled the broadband wire could provide preferential treatment as well. Inevitably, this leads to broader questions: What is the public interest? And what requirements, if any, should government impose on companies to comply with the public interest?

FOR THE PUBLIC interest to be harmed, AOL Time Warner's efforts at synergy and convergence had to succeed. But as AOL Time Warner—and Vivendi, Disney, Bertelsmann, and a decade earlier, Sony—would discover, synergy was easier to proclaim than to accomplish. As the largest individual shareholder in AOL Time Warner, Ted Turner learned this painfully. While he had misgivings, Turner was at first enthusiastic about the company's power and its new emphasis on coordination and synergy. Of Gerald Levin's management over the past five years, he bluntly said, "The Time Warner divisions did not cooperate the way they should have. . . . I think he did a pretty marginal job of running the company." But by the fall of 2001, Turner could see that the ambitious financial targets were not spurring the creation of a single corporate culture. Warner Bros. didn't want to offer its movies exclusively to TNT, any more than Time Warner Cable wanted to air only Turner Broadcasting's cable networks, or the WB network wanted only to sell its shows to its sister divisions. Warner Bros. has an interest in placating movie stars, an interest not shared by its magazine division. Warner Music would like AOL to exclusively promote its products, but if it did AOL would deny itself revenues from other companies, as well as denying consumers more choice. If Time Inc. publications only offered favorable reviews to Warner Bros. movies, they would diminish the independence that builds a journalistic brand. Because each division wanted to boost its own revenues, and boost executive performance bonuses, it did not forge exclusive deals with its sister divisions. Each division was just obeying the tested laws of capitalism—maximizing its profits and shareholder value. Thus, the much-touted strategy of synergy and convergence often warred with capitalism.

Moreover, as Turner knew but sometimes forgot, size also conferred disadvantages. Although eighty percent of mergers fail, few corporate chieftains heed this dismal statistic. They believed, as did AOL Time Warner, that getting larger ensured success. Thus, the push toward conglomerates that had fallen out of favor in the seventies made a comeback in the eighties. Wall Street investment banks and brokerage houses became convinced that they had to become full-service financial supermarkets, failing to heed warnings that clients would feel lost in a giant company and that pressures to create, say, synergies between the research and the investment banking divisions would lead to scandal and tarnish the brand. Other industries—commercial banking, food, insurance, publishing—also succumbed to the urge to merge, with equally mixed results.

A self-proclaimed "rabbit" like Turner understood the danger. Large companies, he knew, usually move more slowly. Change takes time, granting an advantage to smaller companies that are not wedded to familiar ways of behavior or technologies. A Napster could come along and upend, for a time, giant music companies. Amazon.com, which a minute ago was written off, has become a force in selling books. The "free software" movement that has formed around Linux may threaten Microsoft's Windows monopoly. General Electric is that rare exception: a large company that moved with the speed of a small company. The impediments of size are compounded by the limitations of people. To succeed, Turner knew, capable managers—not marketing and convergence schemes—were central. Dick Parsons echoed Turner's viewpoint when he pensively told me, "I wonder, are we building things in this world that are beyond the state of our management? I don't know the answer. We are a huge global company. Do we know how to manage these things? Time will tell. But it is not clear to me that we do."

Yet Turner, like Parsons, supported the merger with AOL. Just as Turner, in 1995, was convinced that Turner Broadcasting had to get bigger. Just as other media companies—after AOL and Time Warner announced their merger in January 2000—panicked from fear that the music would stop and they would be left without a dance partner. There are those who believe that corporate chieftains are clear about what they want and move in a straight line, ever mindful of their own corporate interest. This assumes that CEOs are always rational, always certain about what makes sense for their company. In fact, fear clouds business judgment just as surely as greed does. In a world where technology changes so quickly, leaders are often ambivalent because they can only guess what technology will emerge. As smart as he is, Bill Gates of Microsoft at first guessed wrong that the Internet would be inconsequential. Gerry Levin guessed wrong that television—not the Internet—would be the interactive medium. Barry Diller admits he guessed wrong when he refused to increase his bid to acquire Paramount Communications. The Baby Bells lost a lot of money trying to get out of the wire business and into the content business. CEOs, like the rest of us, are burdened by contradictory impulses and sometimes get confused.

As a businessman, Turner thought the merger with AOL was in the company's interest. But he was ambivalent. When he paused and stopped thinking as Businessman Turner and put on his Citizen Turner hat, Ted Turner was troubled by the rush of media mergers. He worried about the impact of media consolidation on journalism. Within media conglomerates, he told me, journalistic divisions like CNN shrink, and corporate executives may try to "avoid doing stories that are critical of the big companies, like the oil companies and the automobile companies. It's not easy to do stories that are critical of GE—you know, nuclear-power-plant stories. When was the last time you saw stories on TV critical of GE or DuPont? Better to stay away from the corporations—they're the sponsors. That's the danger." Turner, to be sure, talks little about the embarrassments of his own tenure, including the failure of CNN (and the broadcast networks) to cover the Telecommunications Act of 1996, which lifted government curbs on Turner and other media giants.

TED TURNER WAS at war with himself. A member of AOL Time Warner's Executive Committee recalled that at its March 2001 meeting Turner exclaimed, "I love this company." There is certainly a needy side of Turner that compels him to want to please. Prior to an Advertising Council dinner held at the Waldorf-Astoria in November 2000 to honor Turner and Levin, Turner stood awkwardly beside Levin in a receiving line. As they turned to enter the ballroom, Turner pointed to me and told Levin that I was writing about him. Levin said he knew, and that prompted Turner to reassure him: "I checked first with corporate communication. I would not have done this unless I had approval." I'm a "team player," he assured Levin. Such behavior did not surprise Jane Fonda. Turner is insecure, she said, noting that the man who thinks of himself as Rhett Butler is really the more vulnerable character in his favorite movie: "He loves *Gone with the Wind* for lots of reasons, and one of them is that he identifies with Scarlett O'Hara," she said.

Yet when he visited the Kennedy School of Government at Harvard in March of 2001, Turner conveyed another message. Speaking as Citizen Turner, he said he worried that giant cable, television, and entertainment companies like his will induce the

Bush administration to lift restrictions on the percentage of TV stations or cable systems they may own. "The new administration has really been bought by the entertainment conglomerates," he said. He feared that before too long, seven cable giants would shrink to two. "It's sad we're losing so much diversity of thought," he would tell a cable convention that year.

On his two-day visit to Harvard—at a session during which he was questioned by Alex Jones and several others for an hour and then stayed for an hour more as the six finalists for the Goldsmith Prize for Investigative Reporting discussed their stories—Turner said, "I've already been fired, and I probably will be again shortly." One of the Shorenstein Fellows rose and condescendingly suggested that Turner might follow the example of Henry Ford, who also left his job but then set up the Ford Foundation, which is "one of the most influential forces for the framing of issues in the country. You have a life and a future and can use your contacts—"

"I am," Turner interrupted, and he mentioned his gift to the UN Foundation. "No other individual in the world is giving as much to the poor world as I am. I'm spending fifty million dollars in the United States, mostly on environmental and family planning causes. Ahhhhhhhhhhh . . . I mean, family planning is under attack. You know, pro-lifers have got control of the White House. *Roe v. Wade* is hanging on by a thread. A woman's right to choose? They want to take that away. We're fighting global warming." He mentioned the Nuclear Threat Initiative and the dues payment to the UN. "And let me tell you what else I'm doing. I'm very close to making an announcement of a personal partnership

through our foundation with public broadcasting to fund important documentaries that Turner Broadcasting has dropped. . . .
And I've been trying desperately to get my network. It won't be
NBC, but it will start with an N—NTV. The good news? I'm
gonna get my network. The bad news? It's in Russia! I'm gonna
try and help freedom of the press. I mean, I am doing plenty,
Bubba!"

9

Exits

By 2001, associates spoke of Turner in the past tense, offering epitaphs. "He's the last of the revolutionary and creative minds in our business," CNN's chief international correspondent, Christiane Amanpour, who joined the company in 1983, said. "The idea of twenty-four-hour news and global news is his creation. That's changed the world. It's changed people's relations with their governments. It's meant that governments can no longer crack down with impunity on protests. And Ted's business also had a human face and a moral face and a social face. It wasn't just about making money and building an empire. A lot of people laughed at him for his political views. He was bold and daring when he said we needed to be friends with the Russians and when he worried about population control and the environment. Yet today everyone is dealing with those issues." She added, sadly, "He's been shunted aside."

Even Turner talked about himself in a retrospective cadence: "My business side is coming to a close. It's time for me to move on, anyway." In May of 2000, after AOL and Time Warner announced the new management structure, Robert Pittman had tried to debunk press speculation that Turner was unhappy, saying, "I think Ted's going to have more influence than he had before." A year later, Pittman, who was born in Mississippi and has spent weekends hunting with Turner, said, "For me, Ted has a very big role. I don't make major decisions about Turner Broadcasting without talking to Ted." This is not what Turner thought. "They tell me I have moral authority, and that's great," he said. He looked down at his tie, which was decorated with orange bison, and went on to say, wistfully, "I'm very busy. Over the last three to four years, I've created another life for myself, and even if they had offered me the chairmanship of the company I probably wouldn't have taken it. It would require all my time, and I'd have to move to New York and I don't want that. I've got this other stuff that I think is in many ways more important."

Rick Kaplan, who was fired as president of CNN/U.S. in September of 2000, recalled being taken to lunch by Turner in his Taurus. "He's really a hideous driver! He's so careful the way he drives that he causes accidents. You just don't want to be behind him. We drove to a southern-kitchen restaurant. He walks in and you thought you were walking in with Babe Ruth to Yankee Stadium. There were a lot of working-class people in there eating. Most were African American. He was great with all of them. We had lunch and he was concerned about the future, but we talked more about the past. Every time I had spent time with him we talked about the future. All of a sudden, gone from his conversation were dreams for the future. And he was sup-

posed to be there to make me feel better. And instead, I left feeling worse for him. I spent more time telling him positive, uplift-
ing things, telling him the truth—that people revere him and it
doesn't matter what his title is and it doesn't matter what anyone
says his responsibilities are. Ted could sell all his stock, divest
himself of every nickel he's got, and if he walked into the CNN
newsroom, the place would stand at attention."

Russia did not stand at attention. For various reasons—most
having to do with Russian politics—Turner's effort to buy a Russian TV network collapsed. One factor was that Turner's ability
to give his money away diminished as his principal stock holding—AOL Time Warner—declined in value by one-third
between the time the merger was announced and the time of his
Harvard appearance, reducing his net worth by about two billion
dollars. It is possible, he told me while visiting Harvard, that he
would end his association with the company entirely: "I have
only one stock. I'm a long-term investor. And at the current time,
I have not made a decision to diversify my holdings. I may at
some point in the future." He hadn't quite accepted the idea that
his business career was largely over, but he believed that his pri-
mary mission now was to help save the world, and perhaps himself.

First, he wanted to rescue his company and its falling stock
price. He believed that Levin and Case and the company were
too engaged in a high-wire act by pushing so hard to achieve
thirty percent growth, and if they failed, the company's stock
price would plunge. He was worried about some of the personnel moves. He knew that corporations, like people, expire. Of the
five hundred companies that comprised the Standard & Poors in

1957, reported Richard Foster and Sarah Kaplan in their book *Creative Destruction: Why Companies That Are Built to Last Underperform the Market—and How to Successfully Transform Them*, only seventy-four were still on the list by 1997, and soon the "average lifetime of a corporation on the S&P will have been shortened to about ten years." Most of all, Turner was obsessed with Levin, convinced he was the wrong man to lead AOL Time Warner. He thought Levin was not the kind of forceful leader who could galvanize a giant company, that he was too much of a loner, too much of a schemer. He had come to think that Levin had been snookered, that he had traded the solid assets of Time Warner for the declining assets of AOL. Besides, Ted Turner no longer trusted Gerald Levin. He had trusted Levin when each was a cable pioneer. He mistrusted Levin when Time Warner was a major shareholder and blocked Turner from purchasing NBC. He again trusted Levin when the two companies merged in 1995, but he resented him—resented that Levin did not confide in him, did not invite him to his home, and did not provide more forceful management.

Levin, like Pittman, pretended to consult Turner, but by the summer of 2001 he rarely thought of Turner or anyone else as a rival. After enduring years of palace coups and second-guessing, Levin was the CEO in fact as well as name. Leaning back in a leather swivel chair with his hands behind his head, his arms motionless, and his feet crossed, Levin said he was thinking of a successor—most likely Dick Parsons or Bob Pittman—but, he hastened to add, there was "no defined timetable" for succession and he had no plan to leave anytime soon. Associates believed Levin planned to stay well beyond the usual retirement age of sixty-five, three years hence. They knew he and Hollywood producer Arnon Milchan had purchased a vineyard in Northern California. They also knew he spent little time there and worked even when he vacationed. He was having too much fun, and although he had spent a business lifetime looking at himself and others from the outside—"there but not there," like Camus' protagonist in *The Stranger*—in August he was bursting with pleasure and pride. "For me, personally, this is the best it's ever been," he told me. "The capability of the management—the quality of the work, the quality of the thinking. I know it sounds a little Pollyannaish, but there are no personal agendas. It's probably facilitated because I certainly have no personal agendas. I'm not running for office. I'm not looking for anybody's approbation. . . . I'm on a mission."

His sense of mission was recharged after his son died in 1997. When Levin resumed work, he was determined to dramatically infuse his life with public purpose. He was finally able to connect the two opposing strands of Camus. "One only finds meaning if there is a larger purpose," he said. He searched for what he unabashedly called "a pulpit," a way to make his corporate life meaningful. "There's a social commitment to a set of ideals. I'm not just here to make a buck." He pushed for the company to craft a corporate values statement, one that pledged to honor not just shareholders but consumers and employees and journalistic values. He announced that Time Warner would play its part in trying to cleanse the campaign finance system by refraining from making soft-money contributions. He spoke of wanting "to change the world." He plunged back into work with renewed zeal. His personal tragedy was a spur for Levin to merge with AOL—he believed that by creating the world's largest communications colossus, he would have more power to effect change. With such a diversified portfolio of assets, the new company could be bold. With his idealistic schoolteacher son in mind, Levin made speeches full of rectitude (sometimes sanctimony)—about a corporation's calling to do more than deliver shareholder value, about how he would spare no expense to give CNN and *Time* whatever resources they needed to cover serious news—even as he managed AOL Time Warner by the numbers and his journalists feasted on the Chandra Levy/Gary Condit story. Levin seemed to be two people: the tough-minded businessman who proudly declared that he ran the company by the numbers, and the dreamer. Ted Turner's mission now consisted mostly of the work he did outside the company; Gerald Levin's mission was linked to his company.

When the first plane slammed into the World Trade Center, Turner was in his Atlanta office, the TV screen animated but silent. He looked up and noticed that a World Trade Center tower was on fire, and turned up the volume. As he watched the screen he saw a plane ram into the second tower. He raced down to the CNN newsroom. Although CNN was covering the event live, he noticed that CNN's *Headline News* was not. He suggested to CNN chairman Walter Isaacson that both should be live, and soon *Headline News* switched its coverage. Turner went back up to his office to watch events unfold on CNN.

Gerald Levin was on a business trip to England, and for the

next three days he was stranded there. He reacted as if his own son were murdered again. This time he was not passive. He grieved by visiting each division of his company to console employees. He wrote heartfelt e-mails. He wrote missives addressed to all employees that he alone planned to sign—until Steve Case, upset that he was not asked to affix his signature, insisted that the chairman sign as well. He and Case organized corporate efforts to assist victims and their families, and the company chipped in five million dollars. They donated hundreds of wireless mobile communicators to law enforcement personnel. They recruited recording artists and produced fund-raising concerts.

Turner was not a part of this effort, certainly not a visible part. As someone who knew the Muslim world, he believed that there would be no peace with Muslims until there was peace in the Middle East. He saw war clouds darkening and feared that his beloved UN would be marginalized. He abhorred violence, yet would be portrayed as a supporter of violence after a speech he made at Brown University. In the question-and-answer session afterward, he became ensnared in a public relations furor by describing the suicide Al Qaeda operatives as "a little nuts" but "brave." His company issued a statement of rebuke: "What Ted Turner said in no way reflects AOL Time Warner's view of this terrible tragedy." With his own father in mind, Turner had often said that he thought anyone who committed suicide was brave. Now his own company disowned him. He was depressed.

The events of 9/11 triggered another emotion within Levin. Although he had told me in August of 2001 that he was happier at the company than he had ever been, felt he was marrying his corporate and public purpose, and intended to stay for a long while, after September 11 he thought more about how his son chose to pursue his own dream to become a teacher and how he must, in his words, "proceed to reclaim my essential identity." He became more of an imperial CEO. He talked more and more about the company's public trust obligations and less about its profitability. He came to see Steve Case, as he had Turner, as more of a meddler, a Monday morning quarterback. He did not consult Case as regularly. Out of respect for the dead, he wanted to cancel the September board meeting, and backed off only after Case furiously resisted. He grew impatient with Case's constant blue-sky talk of how the "convergence" of various technologies would unleash a burst of growth for AOL, if only the company invested more in technology, a view which Levin did not share. He no longer disguised his contempt for some board members—especially those from the AOL side—whom he felt knew little about the content business and were too preoccupied with profits. Determined to explore expansion opportunities for the company's cable holdings, he went off without Case to negotiate with AT&T to buy its cable operations, which were the nation's largest. Levin wasn't committed to making a bid for AT&T's cable assets, but he told the board that he, Parsons, and Pittman were involved in the discussions. They were keeping lines of communication open, he said, not negotiating. "What Gerry was really saying," observed a senior company executive who was privy to the discussions, was, " 'I don't want Steve at the table.' "

Case got that message. "To Steve, it was all about his role," said the senior executive. Case thought Levin was adopting a strategy, and strategy was part of Case's portfolio as chairman. There had long been a debate within communications companies over whether content or distribution was king, over whether it made sense to invest in delivery systems like the cable wire or in the content that traveled over that wire and appeared on the screen. Case and Turner and some board members were angry. They believed Levin was ignoring not just them but their reluctance to invest still more in the distribution part of the business. They feared that the company already had too large a debt burden, that it would be difficult to digest still another large company when AOL and Time Warner were suffering indigestion. Besides, they feared offending government regulators with yet another mega-merger.

Case was seething, and the aftershock from 9/11 became his ally. As Levin acted alone, the company's stock price fell further—from a high of seventy-three dollars per share just after the merger was announced to about thirty dollars per share. Because AOL's growth had slowed and the country was in a recession, the company was forced to admit that it would fall short of its ambitious thirty percent growth targets. This news sped the stock's decline. And as the stock fell, employees—particularly those from Time Warner divisions—began to voice their anger. None were angrier than Ted Turner, whose stake in the company was once worth over seven billion dollars; by the fall of 2001 he had lost more than half his net worth. The initial target of Turner's rage was Gerald Levin.

At the November board meeting, Turner was seated beside Levin and startled both him and the board by citing a quote from Levin that appeared weeks earlier in an article I had written for the *New Yorker*. When I had interviewed Levin in August, I wanted to induce him to talk about his son but had little expectation that he would. He was too private, I thought. So after an hour or so of talking about the business, I backed into it and asked about the impact of his son's death. Levin was mute, but his eyes moistened and reddened, and the words came pouring out, as if waiting for an excuse. He spoke of how "I was always satisfied to live through my son," but that after Jonathan's death, when he returned to the company he had a "mission." Turner now read aloud to the board what Levin said next: "I'm not a big consultant of boards. . . . There's nothing anyone can say to me, do to me, write about me, that can affect me. I used to care somewhat because it affected the stock price. Now it's his view that I care about."

In his loud voice, the company's largest individual shareholder told fellow directors he was shocked at Levin's disdain for profits and for his directors. *How dare you insult directors when you have led this company to ruin. Our stock has plunged. Our profits have fallen short of your promises. Our employees are unhappy. We have overpromised. We have oversold AOL as the engine for the company's resurgence. We need a new CEO.*

Levin greeted Turner's tirade with opaque silence. Toward Turner he adopted an air of condescension. "Ted always needs somebody to be his demon," Levin told the *New York Times* some months later. "Rupert used to be his demon. Now it's me."

No one rose to second Turner. It was unclear whether directors dismissed this as just another of Turner's rants. Levin knew
that his fellow directors saw Turner as a loose cannon and would
not follow his lead. But he also knew that no one rose to defend
him. The stock was heading downward—eventually to near single digits. And Levin and Case were barely speaking. At the
Western Cable convention a week later, Turner attacked Levin
publicly, announcing that his biggest regret was that he did not
purchase Time Warner "so I could have fired Gerry Levin before
he fired me." These remarks, like those he made privately to the
board, had zero impact on Levin's fate, directors insist.

Nevertheless, Levin's fate was now on the table. Clearly, some
directors were fatigued with Levin. In the days following the
November board meeting, Case called directors to express his
displeasure that Levin was ignoring the board. Then directors
had individual phone conversations among themselves. Turner
was a party to none of these calls; he wasn't even aware of them.
Levin was aware of them and told directors he would not be
second-guessed. Two weeks after the November board meeting,
Turner was asked to participate in a board conference call
chaired by Fay Vincent, who was close to both Levin and Dick
Parsons. Turner got on the phone and was startled to learn that
Levin had resigned and that Parsons would replace him as CEO;
Bob Pittman would become the chief operating officer under
Parsons. Turner didn't know whether Levin was pushed off the
ledge or chose to jump. Senior executives at the company,
including those close to Case and Parsons, believe he both
jumped and was pushed.

What apparently happened is that Levin righteously refused to change, and Case and other directors insisted he must. He probably could have chosen to stay, but he could no longer alone define the terms. He was tired. Instead of fighting or compromising, he marched off into the sunset, announcing on December 5 that he would retire. Levin said he planned to write a novel. "I want the poetry back in my life," he declared.

TED TURNER LIKED Dick Parsons. The new CEO had a scruffy beard and a relaxed manner. He always made time to talk to people, and in a corporation of big egos, he knew how to listen. Gerry Levin humored Turner; Dick Parsons listened to him. Dick Parsons also owned a rags-to-riches resume that appealed to Turner.

The eldest son of five children, Parsons was raised in Brooklyn's Bedford-Stuyvesant, a neighborhood that was ninety percent black. His father, Lorenzo, had a college degree and was an electronics technician with the Sperry Rand Corporation; his mother, Isabelle, was a homemaker. He was not self-conscious then, nor is he now, about his race. "Me, personally, I was never self-conscious of it, which has been an advantage," he told me. "There is something to this notion of self-fulfilling prophecy. If you go into a situation convinced people will treat you a certain way, you will perceive that they do. Second, to have a perception that I'm black almost inevitably creates barriers in your own mind. I think a lot of black people do that. . . . It never occurred to me I couldn't do anything." He attended public schools, was deft in sports, and skipped two grades.

He was only sixteen when he went off to the University of Hawaii, and he felt liberated. "I went a little crazy, I think," he said. "I had a job"—parking cars—"so I had some money." He was a basketball star, and the social chairman of his fraternity for two years. "My specialty was parties." He loved beer, bridge, shooting pool, and music. In his sophomore year in English class, he met a student from Oklahoma named Laura Bush. "He used to cut classes and do no work," she recalls. "I was helping him get through English. We started dating." She is white and nearly a foot and a half shorter than Parsons, who is six-feet-four-inches tall. And, as he remembers, she was as "stable" and "rational" as his father and as straightforward as his mother.

By junior year, they were living together. They would marry at the end of their senior year in 1968, a marriage that then violated the miscegenation laws of many states. Laura Parsons pushed Dick to go to law school. He was accepted by the Albany Law School of Union University. While he was a student, Laura worked as a secretary, and he worked as a janitor at the law school. Parsons graduated first in his class in 1971 and got the highest grade in the state on his bar exam. Staff members in the office of Republican governor Nelson A. Rockefeller heard about him, and soon he was working as a junior lawyer for Rockefeller's counsel. He then wore a huge Afro and looked like a giant. He quickly moved up the ladder in the governor's legal office, and when President Gerald Ford selected Rockefeller as his vice president in 1974, Rockefeller asked Parsons to move to Washington as his deputy counsel. He became a deputy at the White House Domestic Council, which Rockefeller headed, and pushed for the Ford administration to support civil-rights legislation.

After Ford and the Republican party were defeated in 1976, Rockefeller invited Parsons to serve as his personal counsel and to live at Pocantico Hills, the vast Rockefeller family compound in northern Westchester County that was landscaped by Frederick Olmsted, who designed Central Park. He accepted, and now called home an estate where his grandfather once toiled as a caretaker.

He became part of what he called Rockefeller's "old boy network," and grew close to the entire family, involved in their investment strategy, their wills, their art purchases. He was moving in new, rarified circles. When Rockefeller made a significant art donation to the Metropolitan Museum of Art, he arranged for Parsons to attend a meeting at the museum to discuss the terms. An entourage awaited him. "I walked in and see these guys still looking at the door," Parsons remembers. He saw that they ignored him, and asked, "What are you waiting for?"

"The governor's lawyer!"

They were really saying, he said, "You can't be it." He says this with a hearty laugh, not rancor. Former Ford Foundation president Franklin Thomas, who serves with Parsons on the Citicorp board and who is also black, observed, "Psychologically, it is not possible not to be aware of your blackness. But with Dick it's almost a backdrop rather than in the foreground." In 1977, Parsons was hired by former federal judge Harold R. Tyler Jr. and joined the firm of Patterson, Belknap, Webb & Tyler. He soon made partner and became friendly with another partner, Rudolph Giuliani, who had been Tyler's chief assistant when Tyler served as deputy attorney general in the Ford administration. Parsons practiced mostly business law, taking a good deal of the Rockefeller families' business with him to the firm. And when Rockefeller had a heart attack and died in 1979, the family asked Parsons to serve as a trustee for their investments. In 1984, Parsons was appointed managing partner of the law firm.

But he was growing bored with practicing law, and in 1988, when Harry Albright, a member of the Rockefeller network, came forth with an irresistible proposition, Parsons grabbed it. Albright was preparing to retire as chairman and CEO of the Dime Savings Bank and approached Parsons about becoming president of the bank. A year later, Albright passed the mantle of leadership to Parsons. Soon after he became chairman, during the savings-and-loan crisis, Parsons showed a sure hand. The Dime neared bankruptcy and lost just over ninety-two million dollars in 1989. Parsons acted quickly, cutting two thousand employees, half the entire staff. He closed branches and sold off nonperforming mortgages. He ended partnerships and merged with rival Anchor Bancorp to create the nation's fourth-largest thrift institution. For the first time in his life, Dick Parsons had trouble sleeping. In the end, he succeeded. "He did a superb job," said Albright. "His success was in maintaining the confidence of the board during the worst period for thrift institutions in the history of the country."

It was the Rockefeller network that brought him to Time

Inc.—in particular, to Time Inc.'s chairman, Andrew Heiskill, who in 1990 introduced Parsons to Nick Nicholas. Nicholas subsequently recommended him to Steve Ross as a Time Warner director. In 1991, he joined the company's board and became chairman of the Compensation Committee. After Levin supplanted Nicholas and became CEO when Ross died in late 1992, and after Levin removed executives once thought to be in line to succeed him, Parsons and other directors began to prod Levin to appoint a president, to bring someone on board who was more of a people person. Levin would not be pushed.

One day, Gerald Levin was watching Parsons at a Time Warner board meeting and remembers suddenly thinking, "He's a great director. He's got great judgment. He'd be terrific in the company." In late 1994, without consulting anyone, Levin offered Parsons the presidency of Time Warner. Even though he was not offering him the post of chief operating officer, Parsons remembers, "I said yes right away." "In those days," Parsons said of Levin, "he was operating as a one-man gang. If anything, he was looking for a partner." Parsons started in February of 1995, and although Levin was careful to circumscribe him by announcing that none of the operating divisions reported to Parsons, he first entrusted him to oversee finance and legal affairs and to clean up the company's finances and debt, and then to serve as the company's chief negotiator, peacemaker, and liaison to the board. "Gerry thinks it up, and I get it done," he liked to say.

Within a relatively short time, he became Levin's confidant. For years, management of the company was decentralized, and anytime an executive was thought to rise to the No. 2 position,

out popped the long knives. Levin, who was not naturally collaborative, ruled by placating the princes who presided over each
division. But Parsons won them over. They liked his solicitude,
his openness, his mirth. By 1999, Levin added "chief operating
officer" to his title. "Dick's done an incredible job," observed Fay
Vincent, the board member closest to Levin and Parsons. "He
entered the company with the princes running the divisions. He
had very little reporting to him." It was, essentially, a staff job.
"Instead of seeing that as a problem, he viewed it as a challenge.
He went out and learned the business, and people came to rely
on him. Parsons is a very wise man."

When the merger with AOL was announced, there was considerable speculation that Parsons would be the odd man out.
Some thought that he was too laid back, that he didn't work as
hard as he might, that he seemed too placid, too relaxed, spent
too much time schmoozing, didn't throw himself into company
presentations with the gusto others did, and wasn't an intensely
focused manager like Pittman. Because he rarely read a speech,
unlike Pittman, some assumed he did not prepare. Unlike Levin,
he really relaxed and shut out work when he was at his weekend
home on Block Island. Maybe he wanted to run for office, it was
said, and planned to leave. Maybe he would accept a cabinet
position in the new Bush administration. At the time, in the year
2000, the common assumption was that AOL had acquired Time
Warner and permitted Levin to stay as a kind of figurehead, but
that Case and Pittman would rule and Parsons would exit. This
did not take into account Case's willingness to cede power and
Levin's to assume it. Nor did it factor in Parsons's guile.

Although Parsons rarely read movie scripts or listened to demo tapes from recording artists or read book manuscripts or proposals, he was not a figurehead. When Turner fought to keep his role in the new company in early 2000, he would unburden himself to the soothing Parsons. Warner Bros. had to wait for Parsons to approve an investment in a second *Harry Potter* movie. Before approving potentially controversial rap music, Roger Ames said he ran it by Parsons "for some guidance." In signing book contracts, Laurence Kirshbaum said Parsons had a standard response: "I will not tell you not to go ahead, but be conservative." He controlled the money that AOL Time Warner spent for talent. "What I do do is get involved in asset allocation," he said. Above all, people liked him—Parsons was the one inside the company whom talented, vain executives wanted to deal with. "My job is to move around and cool out the younger horses," he said. "I'm the pony horse."

Levin regarded him as more than that, telling me four months before Parsons was chosen to succeed him, "If you wanted someone to go down to see the FCC or the FTC, there is no one better than Dick. And he makes these people feel good afterward. That's why I gave him the content business and people development in the company. Pittman got all the press. But what could be more important than people development in a company? He handles every contract in the company."

TED TURNER WAS ecstatic to learn of Parsons's ascension. "Dick and I have been friends for a long time, and we have a deep mutual respect for one another," he told me. Turner still had his vice chairman's title and little to do at the company, but at least his nemesis, Gerry Levin, was gone. At first, Turner wondered whether Parsons might carve out a larger role for him at the company, maybe give him back a say in CNN's fate. He was encouraged days later when the diplomatically deft Parsons met with Turner, told him he wished to renew his employment contract, and pledged to more fully consult with him. Turner gladly signed on. He had a more relaxed relationship with Parsons than with Levin. Besides, the idea of a black man as CEO of the world's largest media company had a certain allure to Turner. But Turner received no new operational authority. He was happier, but still not happy—particularly after the company, in late 2001, announced the cancellation of his cherished Goodwill Games, whose losses over two decades totaled about $150 million.

The year 2002 brought more bad news for Turner and his company. With its successful purchase of AT&T's cable systems, Comcast now eclipsed AOL Time Warner as the nation's foremost cable company. AOL Time Warner's stock price kept falling. The company's debt load had risen to twenty-six billion dollars. By the time of the annual shareholders' meeting at Harlem's Apollo Theater in May, employees and stockholders were palpably angry, hurling a barrage of hostile questions at Case and other officers who were on stage, while Turner sat in the audience and said nothing. He beamed when Levin concluded his remarks this way: "And so I just fade away, an old CEO." When the presentation and questions were over, he slipped out a side door, trying to avoid the press.

He and shareholders were even angrier in July when Alec Klein of the *Washington Post* reported that since the merger was announced in 2000, AOL had inflated its revenues by one percent ($190 million) and its earnings by nearly two percent ($97 million). Although the amounts were relatively small, there were at least two rewards for cooking the books. As the dot-com boom went bust in 2000 and advertising revenues collapsed, AOL worried that Time Warner would back out of the merger before it was officially consummated in January of 2001. By portraying AOL as a stable ship in a stormy sea, Time Warner's fears were calmed. And by booking ads it didn't have, AOL was able to appease Wall Street by meeting or exceeding its ambitious growth targets. Soon after the *Washington Post* report appeared, the SEC announced it would commence an investigation. The company said that several key AOL employees, including its belligerent business affairs chief, David M. Colburn, had been forced out.

Reports of infighting between the AOL and Time Warner divisions surfaced. As AOL revenues sank, Time Warner employees felt they had been tricked. Their stock had plunged, and with it their retirement income. They particularly resented Bob Pittman's exhortations to increase revenues and margins, and what they came to see as his cold manner. A man division presidents once hailed as a great executive was now denounced as a failure. As they grew angrier, these whispers were repeated to reporters, who printed them. Feeling this heat, and uncertain whether he had the stamina to try and fix AOL again, Bob Pittman confided his doubts to Parsons. Alarmed by Pittman's fatigue, Parsons agreed that he should leave. In July of 2002, Pittman resigned and Parsons announced that two long-time Time Warner executives, Time Inc. chairman Don Logan and HBO chairman Jeffrey Bewkes, would replace him as co-chief operating officers. The old media company was ascendant, and this development pleased Ted Turner. But he still wasn't pleased that his own company stock, which was worth $7.2 billion on the day of the merger, was by August of 2002 worth only $1.76 billion—"I lost three-quarters of what my wealth was," Turner told me that summer. He fretted that AOL had overpromised and underdelivered. "The old part of the company is doing fine," he said, pointedly.

And more bad news lay ahead. With thirty-five million subscribers, AOL was still a powerhouse. But its subscription growth had slowed, its advertising and e-commerce revenues were way off, and for the first time Microsoft's still weaker rival, MSN, was attracting more new subscribers. With high-speed broadband access to the Internet multiplying, AOL had reason to worry that it would become a classic middleman, squeezed out by customers unwilling to pay a monthly fee when they can roam the Web for free, or roam more cheaply. The challenge for AOL was to offer services consumers could not readily get elsewhere. This meant that AOL had to rely on the content divisions of the company—CNN, movies, music, magazines, television, HBO, books—to deliver a unique product to consumers. In turn, this meant that these divisions must sometimes sacrifice their own interests—by making exclusive deals with AOL. It meant that Parsons and his deputies would have to bang heads in a company that traditionally resisted central control. And, simultaneously, Parsons had to boost the stock price from the low teens and reduce the company's twenty-six billion dollars' worth of debt, whose interest payments were draining profits.

Although the media and Wall Street played AOL Time Warner's predicament as dire—as if AOL Time Warner were nearly as bankrupt as Enron or WorldCom, as if the company were in the final inning of a nine-inning contest—this was hyperbolic. Every division of the company, including AOL, had positive cash flow and was profitable. On revenues of forty-one billion dollars in 2002, the company's EBITDA rose five percent to nine billion dollars, and nearly half of these earnings was listed as free cash flow—monies unburdened by interest, dividend, or tax payments. Yet the company was reporting paper losses due to write-downs tied to the stock's collapse. And Parsons reported that corporate debt would rise about two billion dollars more, before falling. Perhaps it was unfair or premature, but the prevailing view in 2002 was captured by a *New York Times* editorial that declared the merger "now stands as one of the biggest blunders in corporate history."

The drums were beating for someone else to walk the plank. By the September 2002 meeting of the board of directors, Turner was complaining loudly—as he had about Levin—and insisting that Steve Case should step aside as chairman. He was the only director, Case would later admit, to directly call on him to step aside. Turner had silent allies, but not yet enough votes. Turner was never quoted in the press uttering a bad word about Case. In fact, he told me, "I like Steve." He looked at Case as a fellow entrepreneur; Levin was, to him, a bloodless bureaucrat. With Levin, it was personal; with Case, it was business. If the noise abated and the company's stock price climbed—if the SEC investigation led to a dead end—Steve Case would survive and receive a bear hug from Ted Turner.

But by January of 2003, the noise had not quieted, and Case announced that he was stepping down as chairman. For a fleeting moment, Turner hoped to be asked to serve as chairman, but the board quickly made Richard Parsons chairman, in addition to his CEO duties. The stock of the merged company, whose market value soared to $260 billion in May of 2001, had now plunged to about $66 billion.

Ted Turner lavished praise on Steve Case: "I admire Steve Case's decision to put our company and its employees first, and am delighted that he will remain on the board and be active because, frankly, we really need his experience and vision." Turner said this, but he was angry, and not just because he had lost wealth or his job. He was angry that the company he had built was placed in jeopardy by the merger with AOL, a merger he blamed on Levin. He was angry that his beloved CNN was sometimes being cheapened and was bested in the ratings by Murdoch's Fox News. He was angry not to be summoned from the bullpen to save CNN, and although he did not expect it to happen, he discussed with associates in early 2003 the possibility of having both CNN and Turner Broadcasting again placed under his command. He was especially angry with Levin and Case and Pittman for burdening the company with unrealistic financial growth targets that provoked a firestorm of critical press and a run on the stock when they were not met. He was angry with himself for selling his company to Levin.

Turner believed things would have turned out better had he been able to purchase Time Warner in 1995. But he didn't have the means to make such an acquisition. And even if he had been the purchaser, by the midnineties he was no longer the Ted Turner of lore. His energy had waned. His desire to escape to his ranches had grown. Some days he complained that he felt tired. He looked older, his hair now white, his pencil-thin mustache haggardly growing over his upper lip, a paunch enveloping his waist. Besides, Turner did subscribe to the prevailing business wisdom that his company had to get bigger or die. After all, he had decided to sell his company prior to Levin's weekend visit to his Montana ranch.

Ted Turner, who had succeeded by bucking conventional wisdom, had conformed to the prevailing wisdom that companies must become larger or wither. Giantism was—and still is—a strategy predicated on a set of assumptions: that a larger media company can outmuscle or outspend competitors; that it can lower costs by consolidating units or spreading, say, its news expenses over both print (or broadcast) and a cable news network; that it can gain leverage over advertisers by offering more attractive packages; that it can become so diversified as to be cushioned against economic hard times because it relies on no single revenue source; and that the advantages of size would outweigh the disadvantages of slower speed. But like all generalizations, this one was an exaggeration. Despite claims that NBC needed to own a Hollywood studio as a factory for its network programs, over the past decade—before it announced in October 2003 that it would acquire Universal—no network was nearly as profitable as NBC. A good number of relatively small production houses (Wolf Films), music companies (Interscope), magazine publishers (Dennis Publishing), and Internet companies (eBay) had thrived. Before they became giants (or disappeared), the rabbits—Dell Computer, Nokia, Wang, among others—proved the value of nimbleness.

Fueling the AOL Time Warner merger, like others, was something else: giant egos. Steve Case and Gerald Levin believed they needed to grow bigger, but they also hungered to claim the world's biggest media company. In speeches, each man spoke of his manifest destiny to build not just the world's "premier" media company, but the world's "most valued" and most noble company. The natural tendency of corporate executives to want to quantify things makes it easier to keep score not just by how much money your company makes, but where it ranks. And as corporate chieftains became fixtures on magazine covers and on Lou Dobbs's *Moneyline*, celebrity-hood became alluring. This was most starkly true in the case of Jean-Marie Messier, who preened for the press in his one-minute of fame as Vivendi's CEO, and to a somewhat lesser extent of Bertelsmann's Thomas Middelhoff, who joined the ranks of former CEOs who became ghosts. Perhaps the drive toward celebrity-hood drove Sumner Redstone, who at eighty dyed his hair a strange blondish color and resisted relinquishing his management control of Viacom. But it was also true to some extent of more reclusive figures like Levin and Case. Private cars and planes transport you everywhere. Aides are always on hand.

Movie actors fawn. Rock performers will appear at your birth-days. At conferences like the World Economic Forum in Davos, you are feted like a rock star. Public figures seek your counsel, and campaign cash. You are treated like royalty, with people hanging on your every word. It is easy to lose touch with reality, to become convinced that, as a sovereign, you know best. As a result, your strategic vision is not vetted—Levin consulted only two of his executives before plunging into negotiations with AOL, and Case's circle was not much wider.

Here's where human factors—vanity, pride, power, panic, publicity, greed, honoring a son's memory—often intrude on business decisions. Because it is easier to quantify success in business than it is, say, in government, the common assumption has always been that business is more logical, with less "emo-tion," less "politics." But in each realm there is one constant: people. Ted Turner's decision to advance international comity by supporting the money-losing Goodwill Games was, in retrospect, one such human-factor decision. Turner relied on no business charts or profit-and-loss projections when he launched CNN. His drive to demonstrate his worth to his dead father has been a career propellant, as was Steve Case's pride when he refused to step down from AOL in the early nineties as fellow executives and shareholders cried out for his scalp. Biographies have been written about how insecurity often drives success. Perhaps Levin would not have pushed to merge with AOL if he did not have an emotional need to convert his personal grief into a corporate cause. Surely, Levin's sudden refusal to play the corporate game he had played his entire career helps account for his departure.

Think of the many corporate executives—Tyco's Dennis Kozlowski, Enron's Kenneth Lay, Credit Suisse First Boston's investment banker, Frank Quattrone, so-called independent lawyers, accountants, or Wall Street analysts like Jack Grubman—who in recent years have self-immolated because of greed, hubris, or cowardice.

If one gets beyond press releases and inspects business decisions, one often discovers that these human factors help mold decisions. This isn't to suggest that emotion triumphs most of the time. Companies follow business logic when they decide to underprice a competitor, sell a unit, pare costs, or beef up research-and-development spending, just as governments logically raise taxes and cut spending to achieve a balanced budget. Microsoft had good business reasons to give away its browser for free if it meant, as it did, crippling Netscape. AOL, in 1999, made a strategic decision to strike while its stock was high and acquire either a content company to provide programming or a telephone company to provide distribution, or both. What looks like hubris to Time Warner shareholders, made perfect business sense to AOL shareholders.

But decisions are also made for human reasons that are not as easily quantified but are just as real. Microsoft is a great company, but anyone who followed its battle with the U.S. government, and the ultimate court verdicts that Bill Gates & Co. violated the nation's antitrust laws, is acutely aware of the hubris that infected Microsoft and kept Gates from reaching a settlement that could have avoided this costly trial. Gates kept talking about lofty principles that he refused to violate, though in the end he agreed to settle for terms he had once denounced. Those who heard Gerald Levin and Steve Case describe their messianic belief that they were creating not just the world's foremost company, but a force for good, could not miss the emotion behind their rhetoric. They were striving for the history books. They had pulled off the biggest merger in history. They had conducted a presidential-size press conference. They had transcended the category of mere businessmen and were now oracles. They were flush with pride.

Inevitably, this rush of emotion can fog judgment. There is, after all, a fine line between an entrepreneur who dares to bet the company on a vision and the one who takes a foolish risk. It now appears that Case and Levin were foolish. When he bet the company first on CNN, then on MGM, had Ted Turner heeded the dire warnings of his finance people and been intimidated by the debt load Turner Broadcasting would incur, he would have made the "logical" decision to forgo these "reckless" ventures. His business associates, after all, whispered that he was "nuts." Instead, he had faith and followed his instincts. Similarly, associates thought he was nuts to give away a large chunk of his fortune to the UN.

10

Zorba the Greek

T he UN and Secretary-General Kofi Annan were grateful to Turner. Annan and much of the diplomatic corps gathered to honor Turner at a UN luncheon in December of 2002. The secretary-general spoke and expressed enthusiasm for the improved relations between the United States and the UN, and credited Turner for helping bridge the divide. He extolled Turner's UN Foundation, which by the end of 2002 had already given the world organization nearly six hundred million dollars in grants. And with Turner clutching Frederique D'Arragon's hand under the table and beaming up at Annan, the secretary-general went on to speak of Turner the man: "I consider Ted one of the best farmers. A farmer in the best sense of the word. Not because he owns ranches. But because he's one of those individuals who has understood something a good farmer understands: if you take something from the earth today, you need to give something back in order to return tomorrow to harvest."

As always when Turner rises to speak, the audience anxiously twittered and smiled, unsure whether he would say something funny, meaningful, or outrageous. And as usual, Turner didn't know what he would say until he said it. He carried no notes, cast his eyes to the floor, and with his back to the East River and those parts of the city unscarred by 9/11, began with a brief tour of twentieth-century history and what he considered its most compelling lesson: why a world organization was vital to avoid wars. He told of another unplanned speech he gave in 1997, which resulted in his one-billion-dollar gift. He wondered why the United States and Russia still have thousands of nuclear weapons aimed at each other. And he ended by sharing a conversation he had had with a former wife: "I came in late one night with one of my wives—I've had several. I was feeling good, had a couple of drinks, and said, 'I really love you, honey.' She said, 'That doesn't mean squat. You love everybody.' " He flashed his famous gap-toothed grin and concluded, "And it's true. I do love everybody. I do. I do." The audience of diplomats and dignitaries loved him right back, showering him with applause.

As Turner made his way back to his table, I thought of something Jane Fonda had told me. "More than anything else in the world, Ted wants to be seen as a good guy," she said. "For some reason he has a guilty conscience. He is a man that was traumatically damaged early on. He went much further than his father thought he would. So what's left? To be a good guy. He knows he will go down in history. He won't go down as a greedy corporate mogul. Although he claims to be an atheist, at the end of every speech he says, 'God bless you.' He wants to get into Heaven."

HEADS TURNED AS Ted Turner arrived at the New York Yacht Club on West 44th Street for lunch in late 2002. Although his role at AOL Time Warner was diminished, at this club Ted Turner was still Captain Courageous. Members craned their necks to see him and discreetly pointed to him; the maitre d' greeted him as if he were Michael Jordan; waiters smiled, both thrilled and nervous to serve such a celebrity. Turner was accompanied by D'Arragon and Maura Donlan, an aide. He wore a blue and gray checked sports jacket with his now ever-present tie decorated with bison. He joked about his lost wealth—"Order what you want," he told Donlan when the menus arrived, "as long as it's under seven dollars!"

He spoke of his company, but mostly as a sixty-four-year-old exile. Sure, he said, he was one of six members of a new executive committee formed by Parsons, but it met only once a month, the same frequency as the larger executive committee he had served on previously. Yes, Warner Bros. was making his Civil War movie, *Gods and Generals*, starring Robert Duvall as Robert E. Lee, but he was spending fifty-five million dollars of his own money to finance it. He said he identified with employees' "resentment and anger and ill will" toward AOL Time Warner management because "I feel that myself." Of CNN he said, "There are certain things I like about what the new management team is doing, and some things I don't like." He especially didn't like that his news network, when criticized by the Israeli government for a pro-Arab bias, was bending over backward to apologize and defuse the anger. "I was somewhat disappointed," he said, going on to explain that it's "to be expected" that one side or the other in the volatile Middle East will always accuse an "even-handed" CNN of bias and news executives should not be startled by this. He spoke of sponsoring an eight-hour documentary to air in the spring of 2003 on the dangers of nuclear, biological, and chemical warfare—only it would air on PBS, not CNN, which he conceded was a bitter pill to swallow.

Having divorced Fonda in 2001, Turner now lived with D'Arragon, the French-born woman he has dated on and off since 1969. During the years he was married to Fonda, D'Arragon moved to Tibet, where she communed with nature by living alone in the mountains. She once got caught in a vicious winter storm and her body temperature dropped so precipitously that she had a stroke. Passing peasants brought her to a hospital, which saved her life and, to all outward appearances, restored her health. Only after Turner and Fonda split, she said, did she and Turner resume their relationship. Turner admits that he does not like to be alone, but traveling with Ted extracted a toll from D'Arragon, as it did from Fonda. Looking up from his crab cakes, Turner said their persistent travel "drives her nuts."

So why not slow down? "Why did the bear go over the mountain?" Turner said. "To see the other side."

Today Turner is exploring the restaurant business. He spoke of having opened three Ted's Montana Grill restaurants, the first of "what we hope will be a significant chain of restaurants featuring bison meat." But restaurants don't interest Turner as much as world events. There was, he believed, some hopeful news to emerge from the bleak events of 9/11. "If you look for a bright spot, it's bringing Russia into the West," he said. Another bright spot: his Cassandra-like warnings about terrorism and the use of weapons of mass destruction now alarmed citizens and governments everywhere. His Nuclear Threat Initiative, co-chaired by Sam Nunn, gained in stature, adding to its board influential figures from around the world. His Turner Foundation spent up to five million dollars and, working with the governments of the United States, Russia, and Yugoslavia, succeeded in securing highly enriched uranium from a vulnerable research reactor in Belgrade.

Turner now spent most of his time working on his various philanthropic causes and traveling to his ranches. After much coaxing, he went to Tibet with D'Arragon; from Tibet's Mila Pass, at 16,050 feet, they posed for a photograph together and used it as their Christmas card. His offices at the CNN Center in Atlanta and at Time Warner's headquarters at 75 Rockefeller Plaza became largely idle. Visitors no longer trooped to his nearly bare twenty-ninth-floor office in New York to sit on furniture that looks rented or to glance at his three pictures of Jane Fonda. Friends noticed that his shoulders sloped more, that his hearing was worse, that he complained about pain in his back and his foot, that he was self-conscious about his age. His energy level had decreased, along with his business authority.

Because of his depleted net worth, he was forced to scale back his philanthropy. His financial advisors even succeeded in persuading him to change his legal residence from Georgia to Florida, where there is no state income tax. But his generosity remained bountiful. He was funding an eight-hour PBS documentary. He was giving the UN one billion dollars, though he would now do so over fifteen years, not ten. The horrific events of 9/11 and its aftermath affirmed his belief in the vital importance of the UN and of the need to curb weapons of mass destruction. "The Bush administration realized they needed the UN, and they needed them right away," he said. "Security issues are heightened all over the world. Out of bad, good often comes."

Not that Turner is an optimist. Everywhere he goes, he carries a heavy burden of guilt. Jane Fonda remembers a family outing in 1992, on the occasion of the five-hundredth anniversary of Columbus's discovery of America. They went to a matinee of a film about Columbus, and in the darkened theater someone screamed out a litany of Columbus's supposed sins. There was a silence, until Turner blurted, "I never did that!"

Fonda reached over and soothed her husband by patting his knee and said, "It's OK, honey. I know you didn't." She told me, "I did that a lot."

Today, Turner admits, "I wish I didn't apologize as much as I do." Because he often says the first thing that rushes to his mind, he has retracted his share of dumb statements. But the guilt remains. A prime Turner motivation, first recounted in Porter Bibb's *Ted Turner: It Ain't as Easy as It Looks*, is to satisfy his father. Bibb reported that Turner once held up a copy of *Success* magazine that featured him on the cover, and looked up to the sky and exclaimed, "Is this enough for you, Dad?" Turner confirms this anecdote, and says, "My father wanted me to be a big success." He added that he "absolutely" wanted his dad to know he has been a big success.

Nevertheless, he remains a Cassandra. At the UN luncheon,

he spoke of how it was "too dangerous" to live in New York, a target for terrorists, and he was getting out of town right after lunch. In a hundred years, he once told me, "New York will be under water" from the melting of Arctic ice caps and it will be "so hot that the trees will die. It will be the largest catastrophe ever—unless we have nuclear war first."

BURDENED BY ANGER, and his Zorba the Greek–like desire to be free, in January of 2003 Turner made a stunning announcement: he would resign as vice chairman of AOL Time Warner. The *Atlanta Journal-Constitution* was so astonished by this, and by the fact that Turner planned to transfer his legal residence from Atlanta to Florida, that it gave this story bigger play on its front page than the announcement by Atlanta-based Coca-Cola that it was laying off a thousand employees. The announcement—and Turner's refusal to speak to reporters—provoked a storm of speculation. There must be something behind this Turner maneuver, it was said. Perhaps Ted planned to team with John Malone and others and make a run at the company? Perhaps Ted would acquire CNN? Or purchase one or more of its three sports franchises?

Like any journalist, my knee-jerk reaction was to wonder, what's the story behind the story? Then I calmed down and thought some more. With his wealth tied up largely in AOL Time Warner stock, and its worth having plunged from about seven billion to just under two billion dollars, Ted Turner admitted that he didn't have the resources to purchase CNN. Buying a sports franchise made even less sense, since the teams lose money and he didn't own a broadcast or cable network that could use the teams as a source of free programming. Anyone interested in making a hostile takeover of the company would love to have Ted Turner's good name behind the effort, but would not expect him to run the business. Of course, speculation about Turner's true aims would likely boost the price of the stock, which served Turner's interests.

The more likely scenario is that Turner's resignation was an acknowledgment of reality. He didn't have a job, and yet the company was renting his name as if he did. His influence on the board was marginal; no one nominated him to succeed Case as chairman. Nearing sixty-five, he was physically tired and no longer interested in being a team player. He hated the idea being advanced by Jamie Kellner and others at the company of combining CNN with ABC News; it was just a ruse to save money, he thought, and would diminish the CNN brand. He wanted the freedom to speak out on this and other issues and to be able to sell his stock or to escape company meetings, options denied a vice chairman. Turner also sought more freedom in his personal life—in early 2003 he again became a serial dater, traveling with various women to his many ranches.

Impatient with the progress of AOL Time Warner, he had been quietly selling shares; in May of 2003 he sold more than half his remaining stock, reducing his stake from 2.3 percent to 1 percent. He still remained the single largest individual shareholder. The fact that he sold 60 million shares at the paltry price of $13.15 per share suggests he was not optimistic the stock would rise anytime soon. (Again, he seemed to bet wrong, as the stock price through early 2004 rose above his sales price.)

Ironically, his nemesis Gerald Levin also sought more freedom. After thirty-two years of marriage to Barbara Riley Levin, over the Christmas holidays in 2002 he told her that he had fallen in love and wanted a divorce. As he had done when he left the company, he was seeking to restore "poetry" to his life. That this was a sudden decision is obvious, for just a few months before, the Levins had opened their Key West home to be photographed for a spread in *Architectural Digest*, which would appear in March of 2003. He had met psychologist Dr. Laurie Perlman, forty-nine, and was moving to Marina del Rey, California, to be with her. He had given her an emerald and diamond engagement ring, he told the *Times*, the emerald being the birthstone of May—the month that he, Perlman, and his son Jonathan were born. "That has a lot of meaning to us," he said.

Like Turner, Levin had lost a small fortune—his worth declining from about four hundred million dollars at the time of the merger with AOL to about ten million. Like Turner, he had not sold his company stock as its price plunged, so he was hit hard and went into debt. To gather cash, he sold shares of his cheapened stock and his duplex in New York City's exclusive River House, as well as other properties. He still receives a one-million-dollar annual payment from the company until 2005, and his pension after thirty-five years of service to the company supplies $350,000 per year. "My needs are small," he told the *Times*. "I'll be OK." As he got older, Levin became more like the impulsive Turner—another Zorba the Greek.

AOL Time Warner, on the other hand, was not free. On the day of Turner's announced departure, the company issued its fourth-quarter and final financial results for 2002. They revealed that the company, in recognition of the declining value of its stock, would declare a paper loss of an additional forty-five billion dollars, and its debt of about twenty-six billion dollars would rise over the next few years by two billion dollars, before falling. Clearly, the company had its hands full. But press accounts of the losses often left the impression that AOL Time Warner was another company near collapse. In fact, every division of this company, including AOL, made money in 2002. The company's revenues jumped seven percent to forty-one billion dollars. More meaningful, its profit after expenses and taxes were subtracted was a robust $4.2 billion. At the end of 2003, the company was officially in the black, posting net income of $638 million.

But of the original team of Levin, Case, Parsons, Pittman, and Turner, only Dick Parsons remained. In September of 2003, AOL was excised from the corporate letterhead, and henceforth the company would be known as Time Warner. The merger acclaimed as the biggest in history, one that would be transformational—accelerating the convergence of old and new media and proving the value of synergy—had instead shaken the foremost business totem of the late twentieth century: bigness is good for business.

It had also shaken the reputation of Ted Turner. He had always succeeded by going against the grain, and now he failed because he did not challenge conventional wisdom. Turner lost control of his company in 1995 because he lost his famous nerve.

His life became one long battle between Turner the warrior and Turner the man who wants to be loved. The insecurity that drove him to compete, now drove him to become a joiner. Or as Jane Fonda observed when I asked why he was so restless: "I say this with all the love in the world. . . . He has been severely, hauntingly traumatized. He always thinks something is about to be pulled out from him. He has no belief in permanency and stability. It's one reason why I'm not with him. Older age is about slowing down and growing vertically, not horizontally. That's not Ted."

I ONCE ASKED Turner why he felt so restless, so burdened. "It's the position you're in," he said over breakfast at the Charles Hotel during his Harvard visit. "Because I was at CNN, because I had commitments, because I did the Goodwill Games, because I was concerned, because I did all those documentaries, I developed a self-imposed sense of responsibility. If Gandhi and Martin Luther King could make the kind of sacrifices with their lives that they did, and that our parents did fighting in World War I and World War II, why couldn't I make sacrifices too?"

Turner retains a sweet, innocent optimism. He has given so many speeches and accepted so many honorary degrees and awards over the years because, he said, "I consider myself a salesman." He struggles to contain the Cassandra in him and to sell optimism and hope, the roll-up-your-sleeves-and-save-the-world kind—like Horatio. He remembers the advice Jacques Cousteau once conferred on him: "You cannot give up hope. . . . The situation is hopeless—but I might be wrong!"

His generosity is genuine, and he remains enough of a ham to seek a fitting reward: a Nobel Prize. "I've thought about it a bit," the ever-candid Turner confessed. "Of course I've thought about it."

Had he thought about what he'd like his obituary to say?

Sure, he said: "He tried his best to make the world a better place."

And had he thought about what he'd like written on his tombstone?

Sure: "I have nothing more to say."

But he did have something more to say. He looked up from his hearty chipped-beef-and-biscuit breakfast, in the middle of the Charles Hotel dining room, and as people at nearby tables leaned forward to listen, he performed from memory parts of Thomas Macauley's "Horatius":

Then out spake brave Horatius,
The Captain of the Gate:
To every man upon this earth
Death cometh soon or late.
And how can man die better
Than facing fearful odds,
For the ashes of his fathers,
And the temples of his gods. . . .
Haul down the bridge, Sir Consul,
With all the speed ye may;
I, with two more to help me,
Will hold the foe in play.
In yon straight path a thousand

May well be stopped by three.
Now who will stand on either hand,
And keep the bridge with me?

"Pretty cool, huh," Turner said, grinning; he had, in the longer version that he recited, got almost every word right. "If Horatius could do it, I can do it. He saved Rome. . . . He stopped the Etruscans." His smile widened, and he couldn't resist a final bow, with a loud "heh-heh-heh." Then he leaned over and whispered, as if to a co-conspirator, "I know a *lot*. My knowledge is my burden. If I didn't know so much, I could just go through life as a dilettante." He stood up and, watched by everyone in the room, walked briskly out the door.

Sources and Acknowledgments

Do a Google search on the Internet by typing in "Ted Turner," as I did in the summer of 2003. The online search engine yielded 394,000 entries, nearly four times as many newspaper, magazine, or book references as his media nemesis, Rupert Murdoch. A lot of trees have been leveled to write about Ted Turner. The walls of his old offices at Turner Broadcasting attested to this, for they were a mall of framed magazine covers about the man with the most famous dimpled chin since Clark Gable.

It's a surprise, then, that so few biographies have been written about Turner. The only prior biography done with his full cooperation, *Lead, Follow or Get out of the Way: The Story of Ted Turner*, grew out of a *Washington Post* profile by Christian Williams and was published by Times Books in 1981. From Williams's book one gets a vivid sense of the young Ted Turner, but it was written before the next two eventful decades of his life. Two more recent and valuable biographies were done without his cooperation. They are Porter Bibb's *Ted Turner: It Ain't as*

Easy as It Looks," now in paperback from Johnson Books (1997), and Robert Goldberg and Gerald Jay Goldberg's *Citizen Turner: The Wild Rise of an American Tycoon* from Harcourt Brace (1995). Janet Lowe has compiled several books on the wit and wisdom of prominent figures, including *Ted Turner Speaks: Insights from the World's Greatest Maverick*, published by John Wiley and Sons (1999). Among the various books written about the rise of CNN, it is worth dipping into two: Hank Whittemore's *CNN, the Inside Story: How a Band of Mavericks Changed the Face of Television News*, published by Little, Brown and Co. (1990), and Reese Schonfeld's *Me and Ted Against the World: The Unauthorized Story of the Founding of CNN*, published by Cliff Street Books (2001). Schonfeld could not have launched CNN in 1980 without Turner's money and entrepreneurial zeal, but this book is a reminder that any birth involves more than one partner.

Perhaps just as surprising, Turner has not written an autobiography. More than a decade ago, he signed a contract with Simon and Schuster, and hired writer Joe Klein to work on it with him. For various reasons, Turner decided to abandon the project, pay the publisher the advance monies he had received, and settle with Klein, who turned over to Ted his interviews and notes and signed a nondisclosure agreement. Turner still threatens to write his autobiography.

In fact, in the fall of 2000 when he finally agreed to cooperate with me for a *New Yorker* magazine profile, as we walked back from lunch at the New York Yacht Club after our first interview, Ted expressed frustration that he had not fully told his own story.

He blurted, "Why don't you write my autobiography with me?" I declined, telling him that I preferred to control my own writing, which is not possible in an as-told-to book. Besides, I told him that I planned to spend about four months on this profile and hoped to write an authoritative account of his life.

Turner opened himself up to me. I conducted nearly twenty hours of one-on-one taped interviews, the most he has ever granted. He urged family and friends and associates to talk to me. When I had trouble getting Jane Fonda to return my calls, he induced her to grant a long interview. He invited me hunting (I declined). We shared meals and drinks and airplane trips and attended basketball games and AOL Time Warner meetings. With rare exceptions—like when he talked about a prospective business deal—everything was on the record, and every interview was recorded. He did not see the *New Yorker* profile until it appeared in March of 2001, and he has not seen this biography.

This account grows out of my twenty-thousand-word *New Yorker* profile, and out of additional research I have done for the *New Yorker* on AOL Time Warner; it relies as well on further reporting—including three subsequent interviews with Turner—aimed at updating his life's story. I could not have done this book without the cooperation of Ted Turner, and I genuinely thank him and his associates.

My byline appears alone, but this work was a collaborative effort. The collaboration began with David Remnick, the editor of the *New Yorker*. He is a brilliant and patient editor; he is also generous: he nominated the Turner article for the 2002 National Magazine Award as the year's outstanding profile. I was honored to win and to have David accept the award. My editor at the magazine is Jeffrey Frank, and his craftsmanship made this profile better, as it does all my work. Many other editors—Dorothy Wickenden, Henry Finder, Pam McCarthy—weighed in with helpful suggestions, and the astonishing fact-checking department spared me from inadvertent errors.

The idea for this biography belongs to James Atlas, who has proved to be as brilliant a publisher as he is a biographer. His careful editing improved the manuscript, as did the deft editing of Samhita Jayanti. I am grateful to them, to Ed Barber at W. W. Norton, and to copy editor Mary N. Babcock. My agent, Esther Newberg, and I have grown up together: she has represented me for each of my books. My toughest editor remains my wife, Amanda Urban, who never fails to challenge me.

Of course, some things are not collaborative: the ultimate responsibility for this book—any interpretations, inferences, or facts—rests on my shoulders.

Index

Page numbers in *italics* refer to illustrations